AGRITOPIA

Stories from rural America and ideas to help it thrive

D.C. Savage

1st WORLD
PUBLISHING

Agritopia
Stories from rural America and ideas to help it thrive

D.C. Savage
agritopia.hfsa@gmail.com

Copyright © D.C. Savage 2025

Published by 1st World Publishing
P.O. Box 2211, Fairfield, Iowa 52556
tel: 641-209-5000 • fax: 866-440-5234
web: www.1stworldpublishing.com

First Edition

ISBN: 978-1-4218-3571-6

LCCN: Library of Congress Cataloging-in-Publication Data

Back cover photo: *Holy Cows, Bankston Iowa, St. Clements Parish 2019. Cows getting a snack before heading to church.*

Preface

My occupation in rural America is farming. My motive for writing this book is to lessen our industries' overdependence on federal government intervention. A teacher once told me that to write successfully, one must first identify the audience. I decided my audience would be people.

So many of my trusted advisors: Farm Dog, Barn Cat and Bottle Calf, wanted me to take a deep dive into politics and maybe even throw out an endorsement or two.... but I refrained, arguing, "But who would care?" They agreed.

Could I write a story of my personal dealings within an overachieving federal agriculture system without some satirical observations on policy and politics and shoes? "Probably not," says Farm Dog.

If you read me fairly, you will see that I am an equal-opportunity offender who tries not to be offensive. I'm attempting to keep a lighthearted disposition toward much of what I work to expose, such as campaign finance contributions, air surveillance of our farms, and what mice know and men don't.

Farm Dog tells me, "But do not leave out the suits; you will need them to help you fix what's broke." I argue, "flannels have to first identify what's broke and how to fix it. Then we need strength in numbers to get the suits to buy in." Farm Dog agrees. Barn Cat slinked away.

Some chapters are just fun farm stories that I have always enjoyed telling. Others are about policy and economics, like fixing Social Security, nutrient management, and the importance of independently owned livestock to our rural communities. If you are a psychology, political science, or rural sociology triple major, buckle up!

Please be forewarned that the chronology of our moves back and forth across the Midwest are not in order because this is not an autobiography. The last Conestoga chapter is one of my favorites.

If you get through this read without understanding my proposed fix for agriculture, a fix that reflects a freer market system, namely the HYBRID FARM SAVINGS AC-COUNT(HFSA), then I have failed, unless, of course, you were somehow entertained!

Please enjoy, I did.

Table of Contents

1.

Introduction - The Fly Over in Flyover Country

Spring 2012. Exact date unknown. The midwest sky was as big and blue and clear as it ever gets. It reminded me of the clear skies we had on September 11, 2001 when all air traffic was halted due to the fateful terrorist attacks. I was surprised to get such a gem of a day since the Mayan calendar was supposed to have ended all this back in January. Darn it, I still have a lot of work ahead of me and no "end" in sight; pardon the pun.

My mission for now, prior to planting season, is to improve and restore what I could out of these new farms. The bank and wife and I had recently purchased them in a territory brand new to us, in what I call the "almost Missouri" part of Iowa – this is the part of Iowa that Iowa forgot. It's not exactly the deep dark rich soils one finds north of I-80. The farms we bought needed a lot of TLC, so the local folks were all smart enough to bid less than I. Almost all interior fences were decent 100 years ago but had since fallen into disrepair. The same could be said for most of the line fences, but at least the area still had line fences which meant it had a livestock industry which is what we were looking for. Deer, turkey, coyotes and coons by the truckload along with a solid population of bobcats, even an occasional unofficially-sanctioned mountain lion or wolf were squatters on

1

this rough land, and I intended to compete with them or get eaten, probably by the banker. (I got my first obligatory farmer vs. banker joke in; more to come).

Old barbed wire cross fences were the source of some of the more dense tree lines. These fences abandoned 40 years ago made an awfully good place for birds to sit and reseed the prairie with undesirables like honey locust, mulberry, cedar, hedge, multiflora rose and thistle. I have now learned that these old broken down cross fences are training devices for the cattle Olympics. The cattle use these interior fences to learn the art of high jumping, preparing them to breach the 100-year-old line/perimeter fences. My first job was to clean up some of this junky stuff before the newness wore off and I just got used to it. Between old broken-off metal fence posts and 3 inch long honey locust thorns, thank God my bulldozer couldn't get flats, because everything else did.

I think most farmers get a spring anxiety that goes, "how are we going to get this all done?" It's usually accompanied by a gut ulcer that takes more than just the calcium in milk to relieve. Not that farmers have any more pressure or obstacles than a normal paying type job; I've worked enough of those to understand pressure and obstacles. What makes farming different is that on some days I need ⅓ of me and some days I need 3 of me, and we were entering that 3 of me season and I well know that after a few days of 3 of me, all I can muster is ⅓ of me. Seems like it always turns into a race with the weather. That's what you get when your sometimes irrational boss is packing a rain cloud, or a bright sunny object, or a relentless wind!

Right up there with the sun, I heard a plane. Squinting, I see a small plane flying low in our area which was quite odd: no bugs to spray, no corn or soybean fungicides being applied, no marijuana fields to infrared, yet! Why is this plane circling our farm, flying so low?

Strange, that plane is circling around our 2nd farm?

In any slow learner contest, I can take first place with ease, but even I was suspecting a trend will have established itself if this plane flies over our third farm.

Sure enough, there goes the plane to the south. It did a perfect perimeter of the third farm, a rectangular 80 acre parcel.

By this time I'm pretty worked up. Could this be the guys who take unauthorized farm pictures and then try to sell them to you for $300, then when you offer them $50 for the picture without the frame, they complain about how much it costs to rent a plane and develop film for a picture of your farm that you didn't even ask for or authorize in the first place! No, it can't be those reincarnated snake oil guys because they don't take pictures of unimproved land, only China does that, and they would be in a balloon. Could this be the USDA, the Men in Black, Monsanto, the EPA, the Mob from Cleveland sent by my father-in-law? Will they come back in a car? I really do like my knee-caps in their current orientation!

Since the Mob or Monsanto or MIB would have probably driven black sedans, and the EPA a black Prius, the only culprit left is the USDA. But why would they care about my farms? I didn't even enroll in government programs on these new farms. I felt violated, then angered, as I started to piece it all together. Since I didn't have a surface to air missile handy I simply hoped they would track back toward the town where their office is, then I'll show them what I think of their "big brother bully tactics." I strategically placed myself on a wide-open dirt lane at the first farm and mounted the highest position available on an F-250 pickup cab. It didn't even bother me if I dented the top of the cab – what would the junkyard care? There I waited and boiled while they flew directly above my outstretched middle fingers, one on each hand. I think the pilot even gave me a slight tip of the wing.

Momentarily at least it made me feel better, until I noticed my new Amish neighbors watching me fly my bird to another bird. I went over to explain myself, and imagine that, found some immediate common philosophical ground with the neighbors! While they agreed about the offensiveness of unauthorized aerial surveillance of our farms, their religion prohibits "that kind" of outward display of dissatisfaction. I suppose mine does too, but a drive through Chicago one time with a drum brake car, no co-pilot, and no local knowledge, I got a serious lesson on how to return that particular gesture.

I have to find a phone number. The Amish neighbors had already employed their phone book in the outhouse, so I headed toward home which was actually a barn/shop/shed/office thing the family and I were converting to live in. The ride 2 miles to the house on that gravel road was probably a dangerous one – thank God my F-250 was a gutless wonder – and if you pumped the brakes enough, they worked just fine. Safely at the house, first get the aspirins because my face was as red as my Case sweatshirt. I know exactly who the "flier" is, now if I can only do my alphabet, let's see, NRCS office or FSA office... they are both in the USDA, I'll just look up USDA, or do I look up "Socialized Farming Agencies"? What did Orwell call them in his book, 1984, "The Ministries." The United States Government page in our little network phone book takes a whole page of really little print. I guess that's how you get to 2.1 million civilian employees, 100,000 of which work for the USDA. Are there even 100,000 farmers left to serve?

The call is picked up right away by a pleasant USDA official. They are always pleasant, until they aren't. I asked them why they were flying my farms, and eventually ended up with a man on the other end of the line who right away seemed ready for a fight – his tone seemed authoritative and I'm sure mine sounded, uh, joyous. I was told they were building a file on me with photos of my sod-busting. This is all true, I actually did bust some sod with my bulldozer, but I was having problems understanding why the USDA office had any stake in what I was doing. I had not signed up for any USDA, FSA, NRCS, ARC, PLC, CRP, EQUIP, WHIP, SMHPP, ELAP, LIP, WIC, FOOD STAMPS or any other government office Department of Ag programs (sorry if I missed a dozen or so). I was not enrolling in government programs at my new farms, so in turn they should have no right to tell me what to do, much less do any degree of unauthorized surveillance on me. I had not asked for their input, or their advice, or their money. New farms, new lease on life... trying to "walk the talk," live a life of principle, no more farming the government, live and let live, leave me alone, give me space, give me liberty or give me....well I'm not quite there yet.

The stalemate on the phone went on for a minute or two until the unkind man on the other end of the line put the hitch-pin in it for me, "if you're in the program in any state, you're in the program in this state." Could this be true, am I trapped by these bureaucrats (derived from the Latin: "rats in your chest of drawers")?

Dummy me, I hadn't seen that one coming, enrollment in one state ties you to another even if it is three states away. When you stop to think about who we are dealing with, it does make sense; information is only a click away. Not that I was trying to hide anything from them. Information is control, and control is the desired outcome of most government programs. They may have started with good intentions but it all evolves toward control. Reminds me of the story about the camel who got her nose under the tent; the rest of her is sure to follow, feces and all.

Hastily, I called my old USDA farm office 3 states away and Director Joe, a super nice guy apologetically informed me that the "unkind guy from the new state" was correct and it will cost me approximately $7000.00 to get out of the government programs in Ohio because some payment had already been issued. Maybe it was the Whip (Wildfire and Hurricane Indemnity Payment, since Ohio has a lot of coastal water and hurricanes and an occasional wildfire on the Cuyahoga river!) By my own free choice, I made an immediate executive re-decision to "get out and go rogue" and I now farm and compete without them, for 12 years now. It didn't really cost me $7,000.00, because it was not money I had earned, it was money the taxpayer had given me because I farm. So I gave the money back to the taxpayer and I'm sure you all saw this in your taxpayer refund bonus checks in 2012.

I can rationalize just about anything given enough time, and I figure even though taking a pass on all this government money makes me less competitive in my own neighborhoods, it makes me more content in knowing I finally "just said no" to something that really bothers me. If this is what they call sticking to your principles, I must agree. Yes, it makes you stick to your principal payments even longer!

Following is the letter I received soon after the flyover incident. You'll see how they accidentally misspelled my last name in the salutation after spelling it correctly in the address section; I guess this is how bureaucrats get their jollies. Can you just see them snickering in their offices by the copying machine about their typo, how they just added an "L" into Savage to make it Salvage. Actually, I'm kind of jealous, that was a good

5

one. I've always been a believer in the sticks and stones adage, but said even better by a buddy, "if you ain't hittin' me, you ain't hurtin' me." You will see another example of "messing with the salutation" being done by a different USDA employee near the end of this book. A trend established.

United States Department of Agriculture

◯NRCS
Natural Resources Conservation Service
503 West Street
PO Box 490
Sidney, IA 51652-0490

5/15/2012

CERTIFIED MAIL--RETURN RECEIPT REQUESTED

David & Jill Savage

To Mr. & Mrs. Salvage

The Food Security Act of 1985, as amended, requires any person who produces an agricultural crop on Highly Erodible Land (HEL) to be actively applying an approved conservation plan or conservation system in order to be eligible for certain United States Department of Agriculture (USDA) program benefits, as set forth in the USDA regulation, 7 CFR, Part 12, §12.4.

You were notified that the Natural Resources Conservation Service (NRCS) would conduct a conservation compliance status review on Farm # ▇, Tract # ▇, in ▇ County, Iowa. I have made a **Preliminary Technical Determination** that you are <u>**Not Actively Applying an Approved Conservation Plan or Conservation System**</u> (NA) on Tract # ▇ because of the following reason(s):

> By signing Farm Service Agency form 1026, you grant USDA personal access to your farm for the purpose of USDA completing required activities such as compliance status reviews. NRCS received a request from you stating that you did not want NRCS to complete a required status review in 2012. NRCS understands this to be "denied access". Denying access results in a determination of Not Actively Applying an Approved Conservation Plan or Conservation System (NFSAM 520.6).

<u>This preliminary determination will become final 30 days after receipt of this letter unless you request one of the following options in writing:</u>

1) A reconsideration and field visit. During the field visit we will review the NRCS basis for our determination, answer any questions you have regarding this preliminary determination, and offer an opportunity for you to provide additional information regarding this determination.

Helping People Help the Land

An Equal Opportunity Provider and Employer

I love the words in red. It reminds me of my high school days when papers would come back with more red ink than black ink. At least the papers came back colorful. Unfortunately it also reminds me of doing this year's cash flow statement for the bank. I won't bore you with all the other letters involved in my ugly divorce with the USDA, but just recently, 12 years after the fact, I realized that in a thorough 2-page July 16, 2012 letter explaining of all the rules I broke when I didn't sign my Iowa land up in the USDA programs, in a great twist of irony, this letter comes from the very person who was bidding against me from the USDA office at a local farm auction. Probably also the bidder against me on the next farm. Now, isn't that special. I will include a fun chapter on that auction soon.

My favorite red paragraph in the July 16, 2012 USDA letter goes like this: "Based on this determination, you do not meet the Highly Erodible Land Conservation (HELC) provisions that are required to be eligible for, but not limited to: Commodity loans/Loan Deficiency Payments (LDPs), Direct and Counter-Cyclical Program Payments (ARC-CO and PLC), Disaster Programs, Conservation Reserve Program (CRP), Conservation Security Program (CSP), Environmental Quality incentive Program (EQUIP), FSA Ag Credit Loans, Rural Development Loans and other USDA programs. Therefore you have been determined ineligible for USDA program benefits." Is that all?

Darned right! And don't forget; Multi-Peril crop insurance subsidies (MPCI), Livestock revenue protection subsidies (LRP), MFP 1&2, CFAP 1&2, and how many other ridiculous programs from the USDA. See how they trap the farmer! They think we can't farm without them.

Instead of a friendly phone call from the local government office, informing me that I was not allowed out of government programs unless I was all out, they applied scorched-earth tactics on me, immediately, without a single attempt to contact me with a regular old phone call. Please understand, this however is not the only reason I am not a fan of the USDA. I was going through some serious soul searching on whether or not I should participate in all of these federal farm programs and subsidies. The airplane experience was like throwing a coffee can full of fuel on a slow burning fire – now we have a bonfire. Maybe locally they had an ulterior motive to run me through the mill, that will make sense when you read the chapter on the farm buying auction – more fuel on the fire. How dare we farmers try to do our own thing without full government endorsement! You would think we are trying to own and operate our own farms or something.

We finished farming Ohio from a distance that year, but threw in the towel for the next, and began the process of renting it out. The renters could then make up their own minds on whether or not to sign up for government programs and they all did, just like the rest of our industry does, can you blame them? Bureaucrats 1, Dave 0.

Twelve years later, going rogue, going alone, going stupid, going off the reservation, whatever you want to call it... we're still here, surviving, sometimes almost thriving. Seven of those years were tough. The general farm economy had a seven year stagnation, I call it the doldrums (no economic wind for our sails), ending in 2020. We did a lot of the things previous generations of farmers had to do to get by. We down-sized and diversified and even small square baled hay without an accumulator, a business decision which also saved us money on gym memberships! We asked for none of the mainstream farm bill programs except to continue our enrollment in crop insurance which costs us more because we pay the 40% the government would normally subsidize (this 40% may have grown to 62%, but I'm not sure anyone can tell us the real number). So we pay an unsubsidized price for crop insurance and get a "55% plan" for about $14/A, giving us a catch net for a catastrophic weather event which I might add is the original intent of Multi-peril crop insurance. We qualified for the non-USDA PPP (paycheck protection program) given to most farms and local businesses during Covid but qualified for none of the USDA ad-hoc farm bailout measures offered by Congress to make up for Trump's tariffs with China or Covid-19 shutdowns.

I feel like every dollar the USDA puts out here only competes against my business. Let me clarify that: I know that every dollar the USDA puts out through an FSA office competes against my farm business. This isn't a Grapes of Wrath story, though my good wife might argue, and my kids are still wondering why all the other kids wear shoes to school.

2.

Get Off My Lawn

This is the part where I lay out the problems in agriculture. If you want to picture me as a tube sock wearing, aluminum lawn chair sitting grumpy old fart shouting expletives at your kids, knock yourself out. Not only do I identify the problems as I see them, I will always try to propose a solution. I'm hoping this differentiates me from grumpy old Earl; how often do you hear him say, "Get off my lawn, I'm encouraging the use of sidewalks!" I want to be the guy advocating for sidewalks.

For all my farmer friends who want to say this stuff, but never get the chance outside the sale barn, or grain truck line at the elevator, I'm going to stick my neck out, and expose the truths as many of my peers see them. Countless conversations complaining about government overreach in farming go unresolved, reminding me of my Sheep buddy's bumper sticker: "EAT LAMB; TENS OF THOUSANDS OF COYOTES CAN'T BE WRONG." Amen I say to that, "less government intervention please, tens of thousands of farmers can't be wrong." A quote I have heard put in many different ways by peers is, "I love farming, but hate the agribusiness side of it." Unfortunately, too much of that agribusiness side has to do with interactions in an office, many times a government office. Examples: USDA's FSA office, County Extension office(pesticide license), courthouse property tax office, fuel tax authority(IFTA) office, county treasurer's office for plates, the assessor's office, the county engineer's office, county recorder's office and the worst is the U.S. post office when you have to come in to sign certified mail sent to you by the USDA office. Private offices can be tough on us too: like the insurance office(w/a 43% increase in property and casualty insurance cost), the bank loan department office, the tax preparers office, the lawyers office, and finally the therapist's office after a visit to the kids Principal's office.

Also, when I criticize the USDA/Ag lobbyists/Congress colluders, please do not take it as a personal attack on the bulk of those who are just trying to make a living within the system, or against those working a day job for the system. One of my favorite people in the whole wide world is a courageous cancer survivor who works in one of these USDA offices. **My criticism instead is of the system's design, and the very few who are involved in that design.** Any personal grudges I have developed only last one generation, and I've become very good at forgetting names.

As I started writing this in 2020/21, 40% of farm revenue is estimated to come from one government office, the FSA (Farm Service Agency), a branch of the USDA (United States Department of Agriculture). I have received a lot of money from this very same FSA office in my farming past and will tell any farmer to play within the system the government has set up, at least until we can change it. Ag bankers would say the same. I am not trying to be holier-than-thou when I talk about my voluntary decision to get out of USDA farm programs, in an attempt to distance myself from an almost socialized agriculture system. I really struggled with the decision to take the Covid PPP (paycheck protection program) money. Since the PPP payment did not come from the USDA office I was more inclined to participate. This should prove to all that my hypocrisy has no bounds.

I suppose there is value in having seen the farming business from both perspectives, previously (21 years) I ran with the 95% of full time farms who participate in the system as the government designed it, now (12 years) I've run with the 5%

outside the system, all by free choice. These stats are not official because I'm unable to find this particular stat on what percent of full time farmers take subsidies. Officially USDA reports that only 12% of farms are considered "commercial" and 36% considered "intermediate." That leaves 52% of farms that are what? I'm assuming bigger than $1000/year gross sales up to maybe $150,000? Anyway, the USDA says they are only paying subsidies to about one third of farms as of 2022. We all know that is a very misleading number and that almost all full-time grain farmers are going to the government well, mainly because of crop insurance, which is the number one subsidy. So, I'm going to stick with my instinct on this one, saying 95% in and 5% out, since I know about 100 farmers and only 5 of them have gone rogue (all voluntarily). All but one of these rogue barbaric types is a small to mid-sized operation, which may indicate to us that this is the size which would flourish without government involvement.

This book is written from the perspective of a farmer and I'm almost ashamed to say it has taken me 4 winters to put it together. I type with two fingers and every time I look at the keyboard someone has switched the keys around. I found out that spell checker diodes can smoke out and may leak out a few misdspelled words. The longer work days in spring, summer and fall debilitate my brain, and after reading this book some may say I never recover in the winter. I'm not a policy wonk, not a professor, not paid by anyone but my own farm and its associated output. I'm just a regular guy practitioner of the techniques and arts of farming, and like most, I'm constantly in search of the truth. My disclaimer is that I am not Dr. Savage or Mr. Salvage as I have been addressed by USDA employees in letters contained within these pages.

My "B.S." degree from the BIG Land Grant may have had a little bit of that involved, if you know what I mean, but what it didn't have was a course on "farming USDA programs 101." I'd be surprised if that course wasn't a prerequisite for any Ag degree today. In the U.S. we have now raised two generations of farm kids who think they are "automagically" entitled to money from the U.S. tax coffers via the USDA offices. It's not the kids fault, it's ours. Farmer/Government interdependence has become such a fabric of the total farm scene that to farm without the government would seem out of the ordinary and somewhat foolhardy... almost culturally unacceptable.

Regarding our farm's journey to become independent of farm programs and subsidies, the financial impact of that decision keeps dragging on and on, especially as Congress keeps throwing money at our industry like it is confetti. During Covid, why is it that big farms got so much more money out of the USDA with MFP1&2, CFAP1&2, hurricane programs on top of multiple hits of PPP, while other small businesses, many of which in our local communities were even more impacted by Covid than the farm, got very little? It must be the farm lobby.

The farm lobby is strong but they are rarely pulling for the middle-class farmer or for our rural communities. Communities where sadly the once-revered ice cream parlor has lost out to the tattoo parlor. I get it, things change, but is this the change we want? Agriculture policies that favor "large scale" ultimately end up deleting the very America that flyover country is trying to preserve. It is my job in this book to give you examples of how farm policies and tax policies are hurting the middle class full-time farm and degrading rural America. I also feel obligated to propose a better pathway for farm policy. Also, in an abbreviated way I offer potential fixes for social security, capital gains and minimum wage, all of which have huge implications on how rural America operates.

To me, traditional values of God, family, neighboring, economic freedom, independence, self-determination through hard work and merit are all archived in rural America and reinforced by its working class inhabitants. The USA was built on a strong middle class. **Why do we allow the USDA to design the demise of what I will call the middle class farmer ($150,000 to $999,000 gross, very roughly 200 to 1200 acres in corn/soy country), an important cog in the wheel of rural America.** I often wonder what rural America would be without USDA tampering, I'm guessing a whole lot closer to an Agritopia than it is now. Let the industrious middle class farmer go toe to toe with the "bigs" w/o hundreds of thousands, or even millions of dollars coming out of a USDA office to individual farms, then see who has efficiency, resiliency, and economic backbone. I'll put my money on the middle class farm any day in terms of efficiency, and I think we can strengthen them without spending tax money, and I'll tell you how in this book.

Sometimes USDA program monies just go to the most politically savvy in the local FSA office, especially when it comes to NRCS funds intended for soil works projects. It's no wonder some farms can throw a lot of weight around in a county office, as we are now nationally (as of 2021) sitting at **only 3% of farms controlling almost half of the value of all row crops produced in the U.S.**, according to a recent USDA ERS-Farming and Farm Income report. With millions in government subsidies going into these operations individually, you can't tell me this money hasn't warped the free market balance, and helped to define the winning farm economic model. What we all know in rural America by intuition can be backed by statistics reported in an excellent brief by Iowa State University, *Rural Iowa at a Glance, Farm Trends 2023 edition*. I give you our state stats so that you can see the industry through the same lens I use. They write:

> **"Large farms expanded, midsize and small farms shrank.** Over the past decade, the acres operated by large farms grew 43% to 2130 acres per farm and production value expanded by 21.4%, even though farm numbers dropped by 13.4%. The number of midsize farms shrank 6.4% since 2012 to 13,500 operations. Acres farmed fell by 21% to only 610 acres per farm, as did sales which fell by 19%. Although the number of small farms remained steady over the past decade, farm sales fell by 29% and acreages shrank by 26% to only 320 acres per farm."

In this study, small farms are defined with GCFI (gross cash farm income) between $150,000 and $350,000, Mid-size $350K to $999K, and Large $1 million plus gross. In ten more years, the class of farms my resident neighbors and I operate might go into virtual obsolescence. Yes, big, non-diversified, highly insured/highly subsidized is the model that wins in farming for at least two decades now. The biggest farm row crop players in our immediate area don't live anywhere near here, and for sure do not put kids on the school bus. Please see graphs from the above mentioned ISU extension and outreach document.

Farms, Farmland, and Production Value

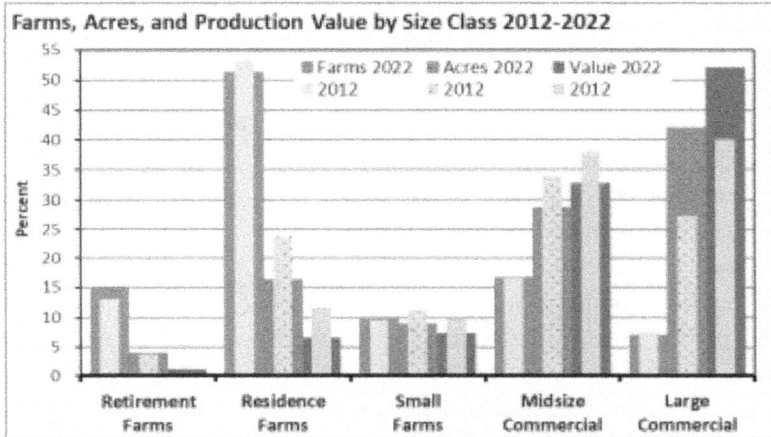

Farms, Acres, and Production Value by Size Class 2012-2022

Most of Iowa's farms are places to live, not to work. Iowa had 81,400 farms in 2022, down 6.3% from a decade ago in 2012. Just over 66% of Iowa's farms are places to live rather than to make a

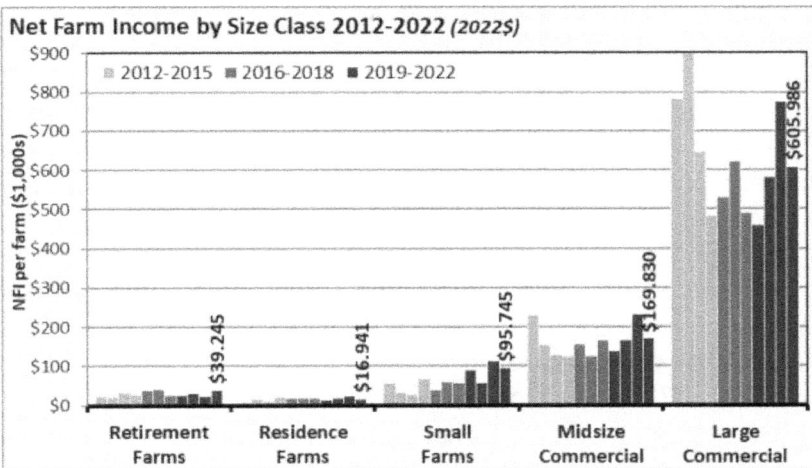

Net Farm Income by Size Class 2012-2022 *(2022$)*

As you can see from the second graph displaying net farm income, you might consider the small and midsize commercial farms "middle class" compared to the income of the large commercials. Farming peers please don't shoot the messenger – these are their numbers not mine! Small and midsize farms do not hit these income levels in reality, unless I'm doing something wrong(oh yes, I am not in government programs). **So for the purpose of my premise that the current USDA farm programs are designed to advantage large scale, I will then generally lump small and midsize into the "middle class" of the farm industry.** This does not mean that many in the large commercial size class live their lives less virtuously, or go around snubbing their nose trying to act high class. It just means that most of their kids have designated school shoes, church shoes, and work boots without holes!

As previously mentioned, net farm incomes will seem high in the second graph, especially to those of us who actually farm for a living. The study's author was nice enough to discuss with me the different ways to figure net farm income and addressed this by providing an addendum to the '23 edition of Rural Iowa at a Glance, Farm Trends. I noticed farm incomes came down significantly in the other ways of figuring "net," a lot of this due to residual inventories, and depreciation.

Another interesting thing gleaned from this research report is in the "summary section" where I shall quote two sentences addressing the cattle business. "Drought hit the state's cattle sector hard, with production values dropping by a stunning 45% since 2012, resulting in acres falling by 34% and farm numbers shrinking by 27%. Cattle profit margins are negative and families rely heavily on off farm income to survive." From my perspective, while drought is a factor, it is the least of our state's cattle industry problems. The top two out of three problems come from an overachieving USDA. Problem #1 is CRP (Conservation Reserve Program) which I will discuss in depth later. Problem #2 is Crop Insurance "revenue protection products" that pay significantly more to "row crop" than graze. Problem #3 is that we are all getting older, and the youth that want to wrangle cattle are low in numbers because of opportunity, not because of desire. All three problems have hurt rural towns. Thankfully, profit returned to the cattle business in 2024, but I personally expect Cow/Calf numbers will continue to stay low in the midwest because of the three problems I have just laid out. The changes in policy I will discuss in this book could really help the cow/calf sector, no subsidies necessary.

Some of my friends are farming in that largest size class and worked very hard to get there, but since most of them are conservatives, they also cringe at the over-the-top nature of farm subsidies, wondering how much longer this system can exist. Farming buddies who have stayed pretty conservative through these last two decades of subsidy rich farm bills are asking, "Now why is it we need a farm bill?"

What I find sad is that here this "Farm Size" data is parsed over by USDA NASS (National Ag Statistics Service) officials along with Land Grant Ag economists, and even Congress, yet they double down on programs that promote "get big or get out." They can clearly see the trends that have developed as a result of government intervention, yet one farm bill looks almost the same as the next. The only conclusion I can make: fewer and bigger farms are the plan... because I know these are not dumb people. **Apparently, reducing the number of middle class farms is the desired outcome of their design.** Who designs this design, surely not our designer?

Government legislators attempted to avert "advantage big" with policies involving payment limitations, per entity, on all Ag subsidies. A well-intentioned but failed attempt by a dutiful Sen. Chuck Grassley to reign in the obvious problems with subsidies. The Family Farm figured a quick way around payment limitations: suddenly every family member becomes a farmer. What used to be a term of endearment "Family Farm" (defines 96% of farms) I am going to have to avoid using, because the modern version does not match up with the old idealistic image. Don't kid yourself, "so and so's family farms" may be on the sign out front, but some of these farms are handling more money than small banks. In fact, small banks often have to avoid lending to them because of the sheer dollar volume of risk exposure, and in reality the banks would be much better off if they had many profitable middle class farms to lend to. Please hang in there bankers read on and see if my proposed solution has merit.

Today, the "family farm" is the most successful organizational structure used to maximize the harvest of money from a USDA office, since each family member "actively engaged in farming" has access to a new payment limitation of \$125,000/yr. for the most common programs, \$450,000 for EQUIP, \$50,000 on CRP, etc. etc. Of course there are no payment limitations for livestock since we made those farms so big, the old \$125,000 limits for Emergency Assistance for Livestock (ELAP) and Livestock Indemnity Program (LIP) are too small. Without payment limitations for livestock there is no need to organize as a family farm, but definitely the family farm has an advantage where payment limitations exist. When you look at the publicly available county "scandal sheet" of USDA payments, you are often amazed at how many family members are "actively engaged" on some of these larger farms. Five, seven, do I hear 10 maybe, it's all part of the game, and the game gets played why? **Because it exists!** Those who play the game are currently winning, and they have a complicit USDA office to help. I say the game should not exist – how many multi-millionaires do we need to advantage? Can't these smart folks make it on their own by now? Just let it go.

Still working on getting those kids off my lawn!

I will have to stick to things I know, like midwest crops, cattle, hogs, mice, farm economics and farm policy, even a little about diseases. Don't know much about cotton or canola, or shrimp fishing, so if I leave you guys out, please don't be offended. I'll try to stay in my lane….and it's from a gravel road perspective with no painted lines. I've gotten an extensive education on bureaucratic/government agencies and unelected bureaucrats, how nasty and arrogant they get when you don't go along to get along. Also, how hard it is for anyone in Congress to make change happen.

It's ironic that so many farmers support the creep of socialism into farming, or do they? I believe they feel trapped in its web. I'll attempt straight talk and an honest appraisal of the situation, mostly because it is so hard to even hear a debate on this issue.

I would like to think farmers could be involved in forming farm policy, but they are not. Farmers mostly agree that farm policy is created by big organizations like the Farm Bureau who use insurance membership dues to create the illusion that they represent the interests of farmers and rural America, when in reality they represent Farm Bureau Corporate and their related companies interests, why wouldn't they? Government operatives who want data, control, and cheap food policies let the Farm Bureau write legislation because it's the easiest way to make it look like they sought a lot of input and connected with rural America. All are wrong-headed and lazy assumptions by our elected officials, who often have the best of intentions.

I am seriously saying to our elected officials in Congress, the Farm Bureau lobby represents their "businesses" interests, which are sometimes contrary to the interests of rural America, so please quit relying on them for Ag policy. The road in Washington D.C. is paved with ulterior motives. Congress, please find a better way to understand what is going on in the trenches of the Heartland. Maybe your own staffers could put out email, or phone surveys like the Ag chemical companies do? You cannot just ask your big donor farmers and perennial meeting goers to represent rural America. What is going on in Europe in Jan/ Feb. 2024 with farmer protests, tractors, farm equipment and all, blocking roads & dumping loads, could come to a country near you. European Socialism in Ag is way ahead of ours and is obviously not working well for the European farmer. Somehow our leaders must be awakened to this fact and quit making these same mistakes. We need a fiscally responsible farm policy that embraces free market principles and ends subsidies. The answer is responsible capitalism, not woke socialism.

We the people also have an obligation to individually let our Congressmen know what is going on out here. The Senate switchboard can be called at 202-224-3121, the House switchboard is 202-225-3121. I'm sure D.C. has a fogging effect on one's sense of perspective, so it might help to leave them a message now and then, they will help you find your Congressman. As one sage rancher friend said to me approximately, "In Iowa we have the most accessible Congressmen in America, but I'm not sure they can do a damned thing about any of this." As he has gained wisdom with age he's figuring there are puppet masters above Congress, he may well be right, but since I can't see them, I can't believe in them. There's only one thing I can believe in without seeing, and it ain't Bigfoot.

My ideas on how to redesign farm policy has no favoritism regarding farm class or size, getting as close to free market principles with a degree of a safety net is my objective. I was once told by a Sen. Grassley farm staffer that my pet project and proposed solution to fix broken farm policy, namely **"the Hybrid Farm Savings Account (HFSA),"** would have to be adopted first by the Farm Bureau, in which I had to ask in reply, "what are we paying you guys to do?" Grassley's office seemed to like the HFSA idea and how it fits into a conservative model for trimming farm program budgets... but I have to go and ask a lobbyist for permission? Phooey on that, it just seems wrong-headed and Un-American. So, of course I did what I was told and attempted this unholy endeavor of lobbying the lobbyists, and then when that failed went back to lobbying the Congress, then when that also failed, I decided to write a book explaining an alternative to big farm subsidies. Thought I might throw in some fun stories along the way.

Also influencing farm policies are government/industrial complex corporations (GICCs) who want farm machinery sales to come with legal protections to prevent the farmer from repairing his own equipment. The GICCs also get exclusive use of a popular tax code called the "179" which allows farmers and other businesses to buy machinery, pickups, and buildings in order to get rid of excess taxable income. **I would like Congress to change tax code to let us share this "179" tax play with my proposed Hybrid Farm Savings Account (HFSA).** Why should GICCs get exclusive rights to benefit from this significant tax play. I don't think the equipment lobby is going to like sharing their precious advantage, but they don't own our Congressmen, we do! All farmers and businesses know well and understand the significance of the "179" tax play. What if farmers and fishermen could use up to half of the "179" to invest in their own rainy day fund? I would love this at tax time. I will explain more throughout this text.

Then you have the multinational, one half foreign owned beef packing industry who convinces Congress to ignore the Packers and Stockyards Act (P&S ACT) while lending an ear to the biggest Cattlemen's group in the country (who has no problem supporting the packers current business model). This results in dangerous levels of concentration, monopoly power, foreign ownership, and more beef imported than exported. Think about that! Thanks to Obama's USDA, along with a "fear the WTO Congress," we lost our Mandatory Country of Origin Labeling (MCOOL) law resulting in a flood of imports. According to an article in *thecounter.org*, by the end of 2015 (the first year MCOOL was repealed), beef imports skyrocketed by 33%. Our own USDA officiated checkoff dollars were used to compete against our US cattlemen to support the influx of foreign beef. It's no wonder we don't want to give the government or the NCBA or the Packers our checkoff dollars. Until recently the government seemed to give the stamp of approval to all the inequities in the beef business. As for the commodity checkoffs (a mandatory farmer paid "tax" earmarked for promotion and research of said commodity as a way to add value) I expose problems associated with them in following chapters and wish we could get more bang for the buck. Perhaps the answer is to terminate the whole idea of checkoffs. What else am I to think after all these years of paying in and we sell corn at 25% below breakeven.

From 2015 to 2023 meat packers could even get slightly altered or blended foreign beef to be marked "product of the USA," while holding down prices paid for U.S. born, raised and processed cattle. Since the country's biggest beef group kept throwing the ranchers under the bus on this one, we started our own beef group, coordinated our efforts with a bigger like-minded national group and told our Congressmen we want policies to save the independents in the beef industry, and we want MCOOL back! We supposedly got the first step toward getting MCOOL back; it's called VCOOL, Voluntary Country of Origin labeling, but despite the acronym it doesn't seem very cool. The packers and retailers still don't have to label where the beef is from, but they can if they want to. Yeah, like they're going to put "Product of Paraguay" on there, especially when that country has struggled so much with Foot and Mouth Disease (FMD). At least now, packers/retailers are not allowed to mislabel beef as "product of the USA" when it is not. Now they just won't label it at all. Isn't this frustrating?

Why would the USDA require all beef in this country (which is sold retail) to be USDA-inspected and labeled as such, yet not require that it be labeled from whence it came? Muscle cuts and ground meat from lamb, goat, chicken; wild and farm-raised fish and shellfish; fresh and frozen fruits and vegetables; peanuts, pecans, macadamia nuts, and ginseng. All must be labeled with the country of origin, but beef and pork are specially exempt, why? GICCs in action. Did Congress and the USDA make concessions to foreign interests who now own so much of our processing capacity that it becomes a **national security issue?** Estimates say 85 percent of beef is ultimately owned and processed by 4 packers, 2 of which are mostly foreign owned by South American companies. A similar situation exists in pork but with more Chinese ownership. We leave the policing of foreign interests in Ag up to an inept USDA with an outdated law from 1978, AFIDA (Agriculture Foreign Investment Disclosure Act) asking for foreign companies to volunteer their information to the USDA. How's that going to work? We need to take policing duties on foreign ownership of our land and food supply away from the USDA and give it to a serious agency because of its potential impact on national security.

How hard should it be for a Congress that is of/by/&for the people to give us back MCOOL for beef and pork? I say not hard. Some say we can't go back to MCOOL because the WTO (World Trade Organization) won't allow it. They are not the boss of "U.S." That's an old worn out song and dance used to support global elites, sung by the beneficiaries of our checkoff dollars. New policies in this country put USA first, as they should. We can't keep giving away nicey-nice trade agreements without reciprocation.

Note to consumers: don't confuse a "USDA inspection label" with a "Country of origin label," they are two different things. "Product of USA" means born, raised and harvested in the USA. Whereas, all meats sold retail should have the USDA inspection label, regardless of what country or what production practice is used. Long and short; "USDA inspected" does not mean "product of USA."

In no case do I begrudge profit or the profit motive. So many innovations and efficiencies are driven by profit motive. The things I do on my farm are profit motivated with a generational bias, because I would like to leave the next generation some things of value. In order to do that I need these GICCs to be going entities, but I also need them playing the game fair. I loosely quote Ronald Regan, affectionately known as Ronaldus Maximus (accept by those who paid 20% interest... or was that Carter's fault?) It goes something like this: "It's not the Government's job to determine who the players are, but rather to ensure that all the players on the field are playing the game fair."

Can you blame a D.C. lobbyist for attempting to enrich her business interests? Maybe not. Can you blame our legislators for allowing the system to be rigged, advantaging certain businesses or groups? You bet!

In spring 2023, I was attempting to sign up for an account at a rock quarry to purchase Ag lime. Short story longer: the lady weighing trucks told me it would have to be done online and I was surprised because it seemed to be a small local business judging from all the pictures of natives on the wall doing native things like roping calves and deer hunting and smiling. She told me their business was part of a very big nationwide company with not only gravel pits but concrete plants, asphalt plants, etc. When I asked if they were headquartered around these parts she responded, "no, Washington D.C." After I thought for a minute it made sense that there would be a gravel pit near the low spot on a landform, right next to a swamp! Really, we all know why a company would headquarter in D.C., because influence and money gets peddled there, and shamefully it appears that it's all for sale. I recently found out the Farm Bureau is located there also, not Kansas City, not Des Moines, not Omaha out here where they get their dues, but clear over in Swampsville, USA. Shame, shame! I found a cheaper rock quarry.

You have to ask yourself: is there a way for the common man to influence legislation? Will my $35 campaign reelection fund donation as a constituent compete with a $20,000 donation from a GICC national concern who is not even a voting constituent? There is no future in our expensive farm policy, or for that matter our expensive debt driven national economic policy, and they are connected. It's high time for Ag to step up to the plate and offer up a new and better way, that's why I propose the HFSA.

The USDA budget is huge and farm organizations rationalize our share (which is 24% of the 2018 farm bill) to be a small investment in an essential business like farming. I assert that this 24% investment warps the playing field and should be reduced and focused more on things like food safety and livestock disease prevention (without RFID tags). Food assistance programs make up most of the other 76% of the USDA budget, and the farm state congressmen won't hear of decoupling the two (creating a separate Department of Welfare) because then the gravy train would be over for agriculture. I wish they would separate/decouple.

Did the constitution provide for any of this? Don't you think it would be an abuse of the general welfare clause (Article 1, Section 8, Clause 1, U.S. Constitution) to give millions of dollars to people who are worth millions of dollars? It's going to take some gutsy outside-the-box policy and bold legislators to circumvent our national economic deficit spending philosophy which ends in demise. Demise, disastrous, shameful, whatever you want to call it, the following numbers are serious: U.S. debt clock ticks ~ $31.5 trillion or almost $250,000/taxpayer as of 1/23, debt to GDP ratio has gone from 60% in 2000 to 120% in 2022. We have a moral obligation to our kids and grandkids to at least change the direction of this reckless spending. Any generation comfortable with the current situation is selfish. It reminds me of a lesson for which I paid good money at the land grant on *life boat ethics*, where you have too many passengers and the life raft is taking on water fast and will ultimately sink everyone, if some are not willing to go overboard and try their luck with the sharks. To me it looks like the federal government is constantly willing to throw the next generation overboard, and we know the sharks are circling.

U.S. farms have been "resized," a product of over-engineering and manipulation by government policy. I maintain this not because we have become more efficient as we become bigger; in fact I see more inefficiency/costs and environmental problems creeping into midwest crop production. All are a result of a subsidized false economy created by things like federal crop insurance, FSA and NRCS office payments, and many of the ad-hoc programs like MFP1/MFP2/CFAP1/CFAP2. All of those were administered by the USDA and denied to the few farmers who did not have NRCS Form AD-1026, the all-powerful "soil conservation plan," which is heavy on plan and light on execution. Heavy on paper work, light on real work. I work to shed light on these problems in the coming pages.

Figure 8
Distribution of Federal crop insurance participants, total harvested cropland, and indemnities by farm type, 2022

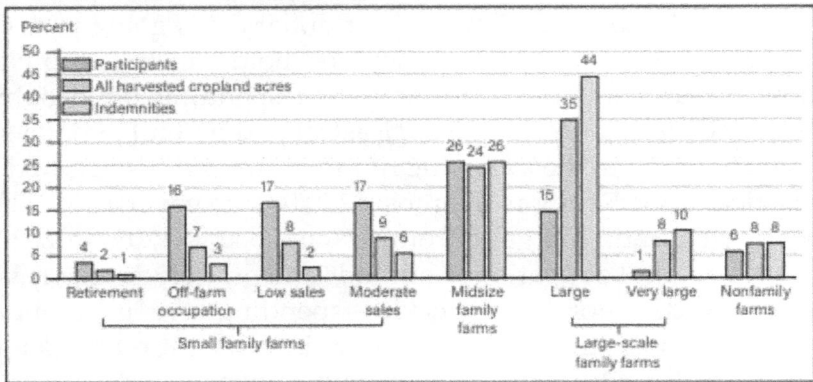

Note: The bars of the same color add up to 100 percent.

Source: USDA, Economic Research Service (ERS) using USDA, National Agricultural Statistics Service and USDA, ERS, 2022 Agricultural Resource Management Survey data.

The bars above tell the story of efficiency through the lens of indemnity payments. An indemnity payment happens in crop insurance when farm cropland acres suffer a loss from multiple perils (drought, flood, wind, etc.) or even revenue (yes, that is considered a peril). If we equate financial losses resulting in an indemnity payment as an economic manifestation of efficiency, the small farms are looking really good in this bar chart, the mid-size are hanging in there with 24% of acres and 26% of indemnity payments and the large and very large scale farms are lagging behind all other classes with 43% of acres taking up 54% of indemnity payments. It doesn't look like the government promoted the most efficient farming model when they went with "advantage big" policies.

Labor is such a problem for the "bigs": they may bring four combines to the harvest show and only be able to run one or two of them because of labor or technology issues. You'll often see them lagging a month behind the rest of the neighborhood on planting dates or harvest dates, I suppose because labor takes off. Don't worry though, there is an open Biden border down south that'll save the day! The cheaper Biden makes labor for the "bigs" the tougher it is for the locals, small and mid-size to compete for land and cash rent. We all have to compete with cheap labor.

The chart below, which is public information, shows the biggest takers from the USDA-FSA offices in Iowa. The first being somehow the USDA itself, and then 2nd is a lending agency. How does a lending agency get payments? I accidentally found the reason in an article located on multiple sites on the web, they say the USDA started to become "not so transparent" with recipients' names, (maybe they were even embarrassed). I quote from one of those sources, "*This year, for the first time, the USDA elected to withhold the names of some recipients and instead released only the names of the lending institutions that funneled the money to those individuals. An EWG analysis shows that the agency obscured about 6% of farm subsidy recipients' names. While that percentage may sound low, they collectively received $3.1 billion — which is about one-fifth of the USDA's average annual farm subsidy budget between 2015 and 2019.*" Does this information bother anyone else?!

https://www.agriculture.com/news/business/usda-now-obscures-the-names-of-some-farm-subsidy-recipients

Third on the list below begins the individual farms they are willing to expose, and the top earners are tens of thousands of acres. I farm in the neighborhood of one of those "bigs" and can assure you there are "different strokes for different folks" as there is no way the local "bigs" are in compliance with a conservation plan as laid out in **the NRCS Form AD-1026. Without that "compliance," you are "not eligible" for any payment from the CCC (Commodity Credit Corporation) as per the 1985 Farm Bill.** A farm could technically be out of compliance on 10 acres and disqualify them on all 30,000 acres they farm, ouch. All USDA payments to farmers come out of CCC checkbooks. Even ad hoc programs like the MFP1&2, CFAP 1&2, crop insurance subsidies and all, they are all tied to "adherence" to a conservation plan. The conservation plan as it is used and abused today is where socialized farming got its start (1985, how did Reagan let this happen, Ronaldus Minimus on that one). But wait there's more. The money reported on the following chart only includes a couple of the mainstream programs, not "ad hoc." Even some of the many other programs included in the second chart called "direct farm program payments" are not accounted for in these payments, what we often refer to as "scandal sheets" of farm subsidies.

Rank	(* ownership information available)	Location	Programs 1995-2021
1	Farm Services Agency **	DC	$10,992,609
2	Agrifund LLC **	TX	$10,509,017
3	Farms	IA	$9,084,391
4		IA	$8,200,033
5	Farms	IA	$7,098,587
6	Farms	IA	$7,082,197
7	Farms	IA	$6,210,323

https://www.fsa.usda.gov/news-room/efoia/electronic-reading-room/frequently-requested-information/payment-files-information/index

Federal Government direct farm program payments, 2014-2023F
Nominal (current dollars)

United States	2014 $1,000	2015 $1,000	2016 $1,000	2017 $1,000	2018 $1,000	2019 $1,000	2020 $1,000	2021 $1,000	2022F $1,000
Direct government payments	9,766,845	10,804,486	12,979,876	11,531,611	13,669,010	22,447,200	45,551,813	25,936,089	15,611,120
Fixed direct payments	18,733	-3,509	-5,348	818	-933	-1,327	-725	-630	0
Cotton Transition Assistance Payments (CTAP)	459,927	24,018	1,064	122	-43	-6	0	-1	0
Cotton Ginning Cost-Share (CGCS) Program	NA	NA	326,456	254	214,562	27	0	0	0
Average Crop Revenue Election Program (ACRE)	255,084	13,738	122	-250	-63	-37	-31	-10	0
Price Loss Coverage (PLC)	NA	754,928	1,942,170	3,213,642	2,064,825	1,945,080	4,952,921	2,099,344	267,366
Agriculture Risk Coverage (ARC)	NA	4,376,992	6,061,419	3,797,083	1,109,009	710,107	1,268,778	117,485	105,091
Counter-cyclical payments	-527	-60	-189	59	NA	NA	NA	0	0
Loan deficiency payments	61,994	154,844	165,850	8,459	-515	6,780	20,949	7,167	3,113
Marketing loan gains	32,955	53,528	40,158	3,440	0	695	78,374	36	5,561
Certificate exchange gains	NA	NA	NA	NA	NA	NA	NA	0	0
Milk income loss payments	-129	-40	-64	-43	-20	-25	-26	-20	0
Dairy Margin Coverage Program	NA	686	10,394	19	250,013	294,551	185,393	1,148,359	128,274
Tobacco Transition Payment Program	646,399	2,574	0	6	0	0	0	0	0
Conservation	3,561,396	3,618,928	3,763,963	3,824,171	3,986,516	3,830,392	3,814,693	3,533,286	3,560,906
Biomass Crop Assistance Program (BCAP)	5,444	7,364	6,879	1,236	236	83	54	70	0
Supplemental and ad hoc disaster assistance	4,725,718	1,800,619	657,543	679,465	915,586	1,447,919	31,408,536	19,010,862	11,537,465
USDA pandemic assistance	NA	NA	NA	NA	NA	NA	23,527,864	7,488,170	540,277
Non-USDA pandemic assistance	NA	NA	NA	NA	NA	NA	5,847,586	8,593,862	0
Other supplemental and ad hoc disaster assistance	NA	NA	NA	NA	NA	NA	2,033,086	2,928,830	10,997,188
Market Facilitation Program	NA	NA	NA	NA	5,127,345	14,202,517	3,781,609	18,456	1,188
Miscellaneous programs	-49	-24	9,259	3,129	2,514	10,445	41,210	1,704	2,156

https://data.ers.usda.gov/reports.aspx?ID=17833

All of this, so that some "big time operator (bto)" can work with a farm manager. The farm manager in turn makes sure he gets top dollar for his absentee landowner, regardless of the ethics or conservation practices of the renter. The whole thing is set up to milk crop insurance like an old cow, from starting with a replant policy or even a prevent plant policy, to providing a backstop for forward contracted grain sales, to getting county T-yield on poor ground, to getting cheaper enterprise units to act like optional units, to getting special treatment on conservation practices from the USDA offices so that the taxpayer can shoulder the risk for farming big using a lot of shiny new paint, but new paint is good for the GICCs. Taxpayers should be furious – I know area farmers are – we all know this wouldn't work without crop insurance. The great irony is that ultimately landowners may be the biggest beneficiary of this system, because "bigs" tend to come and go, sometimes they even go in orange jumpsuits.

They're almost off my lawn now.

The small and mid-sized farmers who gripe about the above charts and all the money handed out through the FSA office are put in a tough position here as most are also participating in government farm programs. I am not trying to be critical of my colleagues, but for farmers and ranchers, stopping in at the FSA office is about as mainstream and culturally acceptable as a trip to the post office. It's really quite remarkable how conditioned the farm program designers have made all of us. I maintain that every time I walked into one of those offices I was metaphorically hammering a nail in my own farm's coffin.

My lawn is peaceful now.

3.

FSA Office Stories

A few FSA office stories may be interesting here, and more fun.

I spent some time as a crop insurance adjuster and one day needed to collect information for a claim at a county FSA office somewhere in Ohio. While hunting down this office in the days before GPS mapping software and smartphones (yes, kids, we used to function without cell phones,) I spied the USDA sign I was looking for and pulled into the office drive. I made the mistake of pulling around to the back lower level and immediately thought, "What's wrong with this picture?" I'm seeing old minivans with missing hubcaps and economy cars with very little value left in them. Instinctively I knew these are not farmer vehicles. It slowly dawned on me, oh yes, this might be the WIC/Food Stamp/Food Assistance part of the USDA – you don't see that very often. I must reason through my confusion: do I walk in here or find another more suitable entrance for farmers? So I drove around to the top front of the building and was comforted to see a big diesel pickup idling in the cold parking lot with no one in it. Obviously this trusting soul must be a farmer who didn't want to come back out to a cold truck or maybe the starter motor was toast (wonder if idling hurt his Carbon Intensity "C.I." score) – now I have found the part of the

USDA I was looking for. Isn't that ironic, I thought, we farmers going to the same well, yet feeling on a different plane, just like this office building was built. What a strategic mistake to build an FSA office this way, I haven't seen a USDA office designed like this since, but then again I don't include USDA offices on my AAA TripTiks.

I can't say I dropped out of USDA programs that minute, but a degree of guilt descended upon me. Ever since, I cringe while looking at that big presidential portrait in those offices, almost as they are saying to me, deal with this office, then worship at my altar. I know they are government offices, but can't we defund the stinkin' portraits! We all know what the president looks like and the people who don't are probably out wading in a mountain stream with salmon jumping into one hand and a cold mountain brew in the other, absolutely no need for a government office. How could I be so critical of the welfare state created by those in government who want collective control and power while blindly walking into the other end of that same office? It's the same bureaucracy. The people who design these systems to trap the masses are not stupid, but the people who designed that office building sure were.

Here's another FSA story, this one from Iowa. Still raw from being harassed by the USDA-Air Surveillance Squadron and all the nasty letters associated with my divorce from the USDA, I involuntarily knew a lot about what was required of me to get "conservation compliant" so that Form AD-1026 could magically unlock CCC funds. For example, one field of 97 acres would need 20 some waterways installed to be compliant. See map below for a visual on this particular farm and please do not laugh at me for buying such a rough farm. It's a great farm for crops, cattle, and logs.

It's ironic that the conservation plan made no mention of any requirement to no-till said field, which really puzzles me. So I voluntarily traded in some waterways for no-till, 12 years now with much success holding the soil. I have a good planter set up to no-till, so that's what I did of my own free will, and complemented it with my own buffer strips, also hay strips which connected my own waterways, about 12 of them. I also plant on a contour, and most of the time plant a cover crop for grazing purposes. All that stuff adds up to a level above and beyond what is customary in the area. It may not be the fastest way to slap a crop in the ground, but that is the way I roll of my own free will. Not to be self-righteous (because those who are self-righteous are right selfish), but I do take soil conservation seriously because we should leave this land better than we found it – a lot of that is accomplished just by no-till alone.

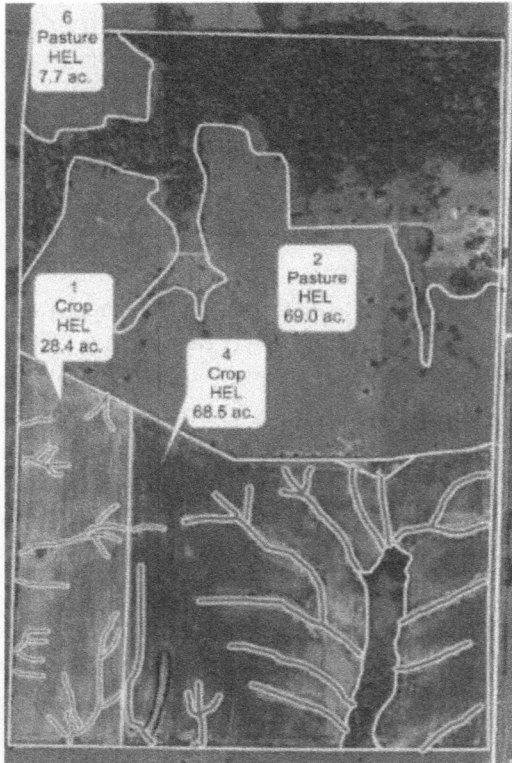

A somewhat brief explanation of **no-till** may be appropriate here as it describes a technique in farming thought not possible when I was a kid playing in the creek. You won't believe it from its name, but this technique allows us to do "no" tillage. We plant straight through last year's above ground crop residue right into the unprepared soil! Yup, you can park the moldboard plow, the chisel plow, the disk, the field cultivator, the harrow, the crumbler, the turbo till, the disc-o-vator, and those other thing-a-ma-jigs in rusty row, designating them for emergency use only.

No-till planter setups vary greatly, but most generally only disturb the soil at seed placement width and depth, so an inch or two wide by an inch or two deep. Most of us in hill county try to leave as much residue snug up to the seed to avoid having a heavy rain trenching out our seed – that is why I have to stay pretty religious about planting across or at least at an angle to hill slopes which describes the art of contouring. Contouring takes extra time, and may even look a little sloppy with crooked rows and all, because a human is actually turning the steering wheel or at least deciding where to place rows so that every row becomes a water break. Between that reality and early weed pressure skeletons "dying off," no-till gets labeled "farm ugly" and despite its great soil conservation attributes gets shunned by that absentee landlord who just left the manicured lawn at the condominium to drive out in the country for a farm inspection. Straight rows rule the midwest now with autosteer GPS setting a nice straight AB line down a long fencerow, making it far easier to plant a field with the expectation of straight rows... even if they are straight up and down the hills!

No-till practices started in the late 70s and today is used on slightly less than 30% of U.S. crops. The technique saves soil and fuel but may cost a little more for herbicides, and my experience shows a 10-15 (4-7%) bushel penalty in corn yield (not real popular when trying to build a high yield crop insurance A.P.H.) but very competitive with other systems for soybean yield. With carbon sequestration being such a big topic of the day, no-till is poised to provide a theoretical advantage, but if we gauge carbon sequestration by % increases in soil Organic Matter, I am not impressed. Disappointing increases, if any, have been seen after using the system 12 years here and 10 years there and 7 years at another farm. Guess I need to stay on one farm longer before Jill gets us kicked off!

One of the neat things about no-till is watching the worm populations build back better and make soil great again. In Ohio and Dubuque County, Iowa, we had deeper soils where the night crawler (big fishing worm size) worms could get deep enough to thrive (3-6 feet) and then set up camp after a few years with these debris food piles over top of their holes called middens. In nature's own random way, they put three of these middens per square foot. That spatial geometry of the hole allows them to keep their posterior in the hole while getting together, if you know what I mean. They crawl around in the middle of the night or after rains with that bulging band patch-like thing near their front doing something to make more baby worms. It is very hard to catch them in the act, as they can feel the ground moving as you sneak toward them. Since they are already partly in the hole, bam! They are gone in a flash, like teenagers on a back dirt road. Stamp your foot on the ground after a rain and hear the worms and water going up and down in the soil profile, man is that neat. These worms and the red worms and for that matter fungi and other microorganisms are doing our tillage for us, and it is amazing how resilient these soils become because of the livestock growing under our feet.

In the "tip of the day" department: if you like to fish for walleye and ever get a chance to fish a double worm harness, hook the night crawlers near their posteriors so that the patches can reach each other, it will turn the fish on – unless you're on the Cuyahoga where the floating plastic pollution may or may not have tampered with the sex drive of the fish, and maybe even the worms. Once upon a time on the St. Clair River/Lake Big ship channel, the guys in my fishing group didn't believe me about the worm rigging. Yes, indeed, they started to mock me, but as I kept pulling in one walleye after another I subtly noticed they got to rigging their hooks a little differently. You know the old saying, "imitation is the best form of flattery." I told them to change their perspective and that "the suck in northern midwest walleye fishing could once again be short for 'success'." Of course that great experience occurred the year before our fishing group's perspective went sour and unofficially declared the Northern midwest lake walleye population extinct.

Lastly on earthworms: believe it or not, after 12 years of no-till in southern Iowa I can tell you there are soils in the U.S. a night crawler cannot inhabit because of an impenetrable clay layer in that top foot of soil. Red worms abound in my southern Iowa no-till, but night crawlers, not so much except in or near sod ditches.

Back to conservation compliance. During that first year in Southern Iowa I found myself ducking a lot – I'm expecting to get buzzed by a plane from the USDA-Air Surveillance Squad documenting farms not following conservation plans, but every time it was only a buzzard. As dumb as I am, I could see literally no one was conservation-compliant to the letter of the law. No one had 20+ waterways in a 97 acre field. Where are the waterways, where's the 30% residue cover, where's the buffer strips down the end rows, where's the contouring, where's the true no-till? Most of all, where's the plane? No planes are flying except the late summer crop dusters, so how could it be that everyone is getting money from the FSA office? Obviously this prompted a call clear to the top of state USDA officials and I got an interesting reply. I asked, "Why is it that all of this non-compliance is tolerated, yet you fly me when I don't even want your money?" The kind gentleman answered, "First, if you see someone who is out of compliance, turn them in. Second, it's frustrating, but when we try to enforce and deny payments we almost always get a call with 'push-back' from a Congressman. So call and tell your congressman to let us do our job."

I didn't see that one coming and it leaves me again concluding that it should all just stop, especially since government agencies like the NRCS (a division of the USDA) are never accountable, and most of their employees are like the rest of us and take the path of least resistance. They want neighbors to narc on neighbors before they will take action on non-compliance, phooey on that! The NRCS is failing to deliver soil conservation, while the FSA office is doing a good job of handing out taxpayer money. If the taxpayer is not getting soil conservation out of government involvement in farming, then why do we spend money on the NRCS offices at all? Soil conservation would be improved without the USDA being involved, and I will continue to lay out that case in future stories.

Time for a third short FSA story inside a long story. In a loose colloquial way from a "very good" source whose brother knew someone who knew a former state administrator of USDA programs, I do hereby approximately quote, "We have the Republican farmers right where we want them: eating out of our hand." Obviously, said administrator was a Democrat, this one proud as a peacock that they were able to have some control of the waskly wepublicans (there's Elmer Fudd when you need him).

What are we getting out of these offices, if it is not conservation? An FDR type jobs-works project? Control of data and information for insider global elites to make money trading commodities? Stability of food supply? Cheap food? Design of farm size, so there are fewer individuals to deal with, or fewer to buy out?

It can't be stability: if you believe in the free market, the food supply will be stable with fluctuations in price just like we have now, with or without government involvement. It can't be cheap food because in 2024, just about every commodity is being sold for a loss and the grocery store is very expensive, plus 30-40% of U.S. food is thrown out, so as our Appalachian buddies say, "that dog don't hunt." None of the other reasons to have the USDA involved in farming justify taxpayer investment especially in a deficit economy. Every employee I ever met in these USDA offices is smart and capable and would have value in the private sector. Their challenge would be to match the benefit package, especially since Obamacare let private companies off the hook for health care. Just think of the savings for the Treasury to shutter these offices in every county, in every state in the USA and that whole FSA division in D.C. and/or Kansas City. Control of information/data and "job works" seem to be the driving factors of USDA involvement.

Of course, none of the changes I propose could be done overnight. To shift reliance away from an over-the-top crop insurance system to a catastrophic philosophy coupled with an HFSA may take 4 or 5 years to fully accomplish. People who aren't intimately familiar with farming might be concerned that land would go unfarmed if these programs go away. Don't worry, it will get farmed at least as much as the market will bear, just like it did 20 years ago (before revenue crop insurance), and 40 years ago (before CCC payments were tied to Form Ad-1026 conservation plans), and 80 years ago (during WW2), and 120 years ago (before tractors).

4.

Can We Evolve Farm Policy? A Different Path: the HFSA

We can evolve farm policy rather simply, but apparently not via the normal farm bill mechanism which has been stuck doing just about the same thing for at least a generation. I believe the answer lies in a revision of tax code, something that gets done all the time. Simply give farmers a new tax play that helps them design their own rainy day fund. As I lay out this HFSA idea in the next few chapters I will try not to bore you, so I'm purposefully going to cut it up with some stories.

Not to diminish the difficulty of any other profession, but ours has this unavoidable love/hate relationship with Mother Nature. It takes a hard headed rugged individual to pursue many of the ventures on the farm. We are all used to being humbled by Mother Nature's ups and downs. No one figured out how to take the dirt and risk out of a lot of our jobs, and never will. The dust and sweat on those hottest summer days never felt so bad as when you are losing money doing it, watching a year's worth of hope turn hopeless, often through no fault of our own. Our livelihoods are dependent on the weather. Farmers and ranchers need a mechanism to help soften the blow of a bad turn of weather events. **The question is: how do you do that while**

minimizing the determination of winners and losers, yet still provide a safety net upon which free markets can function?

A subsidized crop insurance system has been the end-all and be-all for risk management, but its fault is that it has become the mechanism upon which "advantage big" leverages itself. It's the elephant in the room, the thing that allows risk to be transferred and margins to be locked, unlike almost any other business in the USA. It's time to push for an evolution in farm policy. A policy that should be aimed at saving the last of the **middle class** farmers and independent ranchers, and in so doing, save the rural communities tied to these types. Don't expect me to ask for acreage control mechanisms or parity pricing or buyouts, all of that would take a USDA office and that makes me break out in hives. In my mind USDA stands for U-Suck (at)Doing-Anything, except maybe the food safety part of it.

Everything has an acronym, if you haven't noticed. My good brother and I were going to start a group for "Farmers Against Government Subsidies" but neither of us could get enthused about the acronym.

We need a system designed to get the taxpayer off the hook and let the free market have more influence. We need to accomplish all this without hundreds of pages of farm bill. We need to chase acres away from overproduced corn and soy back to their more native and appropriate use in pasture, hay, small grains, fallow, maybe even to buffers, wetlands, wastelands and woods. Subsidies and Revenue Protection crop insurance only get in the way of this simple land use dynamic while at the same time contributing to our biggest cost, the cost of land. Again, I assert that **there has never been a government farm program that did not end up getting passed down the line ultimately into the landowner's pocket.** Many Congressmen are landowners and support the status-quo farm programs that have consolidated land into fewer and fewer hands. Crop insurance has allowed the rents to be raised, advantaging the non-farming landowners who Iowa State University says now own 68% of Iowa land, as of 2021.

The idea I am promoting gives the farmer/rancher/fisherman an **HFSA - a tax advantaged savings account, not just a regular**

savings account implementable by a simple alteration in tax code. An idea hatched while doing cattle chores, not totally unique in a larger sense but probably unique in how it hybridizes existing tax plays. I call it hybrid because we would need to tap into three concepts which already exist in tax law by:

1. **stealing the framework of an HSA (health savings accounts)**
2. **alter the "section 179" to allow up to half of it to go into the HFSA**
3. **allowing the account to function as an IRA in retirement.**

Couple this with catastrophic multi peril crop insurance coverage which already exists from private companies and off we go. New system.

Simple, aye?

I've not been able to get help from any big organization to promote this as an alternate pathway for the farm, but from the response of my peers, it withstands most of their criticisms and harsh reviews. I think the HFSA is capable of addressing the problem of a false economy created by a highly subsidized system. This account must have liquidity: money must be accessible whether being removed as a tax-free distribution or taxed distribution but always with no penalties. Coupled with un-subsidized catastrophic crop insurance it creates a self-directed rainy day fund for farmers, delivering that needed free market reactivity, eventually replacing big farm programs designed by Congress every 4 years. Even ad-hoc programs could then be a thing of the past.

By allowing up to ½ of Section 179 depreciation (farmers' most popular tax shelter) or up to $20,000/yr. into this account, young "wanna-be" farmers could start putting together a tax deferred batch of equity helping them secure credit, while old farmers like me could be putting it away for a bad year, or retirement. Money could come out of this account tax free when the governor of your state declares a "disaster area" encompassing your farm's geography. Money could also be pulled out of this account even in a good year, subject to taxation at your regular rate, a feature handy for income averaging. I will go into more detail later along with the stories of promoting this concept locally at Farm Bureau meetings and in Washington D.C.

Since this is not just a book about economics I will now dive into some lighter farm life related stories with levity involved. Some of these stories are topical and help explain my previous assertions, others are just fun farm related stories.

5.

Personal Trek and Places We Have Farmed

I'll touch briefly on places we have farmed, not to be autobiographical but to paint a background and give you a little perspective. Plus, my kids said, "Dad, you have to have more than 10 pages if you're going to write a book."

I was raised on a part-timer's farm in southern Ohio, 88 acres of mostly tillable and hay. It also had a big white post and beam barn with an awesome creek where fossil stones showed up in the dry months. The farm was smaller than most full-time farms of that era, but bigger than a hobby farm. We always had cows and always did the hay on that farm, and some big sweet corn patches for a roadside market, but didn't start row cropping until I was a freshman in high school when the sharecropper man decided to retire. The two boys of the family loved anything machine or cow, and the girls were capable but reluctant to run a machine, but sometimes had to, especially to pull the grain drill or hay rake. It was a perfect place for all the kids to learn while doing and I really appreciate that Dad was willing to turn some of us loose on many of those simple old pieces of farm equipment.

I had 8 siblings to compete with for green beans and liver

at the supper table. Amish/Catholic is as close as I can describe the religious and socio-economic model of my upbringing. Food was never scarce. Oversimplifying here, Dad was a great provider and never got sick enough to miss a day at work. Mom cleaned a lot of cloth diapers and packed a lot of lunches and organized a lot of meals and prayers. She also had a big garden and did plenty of canning. God Bless her, I hope she got a new pressure cooker in heaven! Thanks to the youngest two kids of any lot, we always had eggs, now and then even mystery eggs! Mom's work was never done – she was the ring leader for the household circus and even helped keep the church organized.

Dad farmed a lot in the dark after teaching school all day. He had this weird night vision thing going on, I guess from his time in the Army, except he didn't need night vision goggles. Both raised in the city, how Mom and Dad did it all while starting a farm from scratch and raising all of us is amazing, but generally speaking and again oversimplifying, their generation was tough and a little less distracted by smartphones and such. I can assure you they did not get anything handed to them from the depression era generation that came before them, so they were starting from scratch and scratching to start. All the kids were helpers; shifts were taken by all seven sisters with "kitchen days" and "barn days." Boys got the luxury of barn days every day. The girls always helped on small square bales of hay and straw, which were very important to our home farm. Mom did get a break from haying, as most moms did. A buddy told me his mom even developed an excuse for this, saying, "you guys do the hay'n and I'll do the pray'n."

As kids we all played outside a lot, boys more than girls, but girls got much smarter because of their freedom and desire to read recreationally. (Hey, this book could be considered recreational reading!) I would say we all profited from a degree of neglect, especially my little brother and me. I know Mom cared about us, but I'm not so sure she ever really checked in on us a lot. She knew we would usually be playing near the creek, or in the awesome big white barn, or king of the mountain on the pond spoil pile, or fishing, or as we got older, wrenching in the garage. Whatever the opposite of helicopter parenting was, but with an attentive and present and responsible set of parents, that's what I had. I really appreciate having had the privilege of being raised by that 88 acre farm property.

The town newspaper was the Star-Republican and the High School mascot was a Wildcat with the same colors as the Kentucky Wildcats. You might say there was a lot of rugged individualism around the old hometown. One of our many fun history teachers while covering the Great Depression taught us the "D" in FDR stood for "Deficit," a problem still haunting us today. Conservatism was more than just a political point of view, it was a way of life: we saved our brown bags from Mom's packed school lunch and no one laughed at us, at least I don't think they did. Mom and Dad couldn't throw out milk cartons and soup cans very easily, they could always be reused to store something: nuts/bolts/fittings/used roofing nails, you name it. They were into repurposing before it was cool. I don't suppose being born and raised soon after the Great Depression had anything to do with that!

I was "out the door (of high school) in '84" and so were a lot of farmers. Interest rates were sky high and a farm bubble had burst in about 1982. By 1984 and for the next 5 or 6 years many farmers were going bankrupt. I followed the old share cropper's advice when he said, "They can take your pickup, they can take your farm, but they can't take your education." It took me a lot of years to figure out who "they" are, but I'm onto them now. I didn't stay around the hometown, not just because I wasn't tough enough to farm crawdad soils, but also because there wasn't a multi-generational plantation farm from which to anchor. I worked at an apple orchard and a neighbor's farm in high school and Dad let me use his equipment to farm my own little 13 acre rented piece of land from my buddy's dad who had enough guts to let a high school rookie farm it. By the end of high school, at $4 - $5/hr. wages I'd saved enough to buy a 4 year old car and at least a year at college, but that's before colleges had a license to steal and the *"Defund the Colleges"* movement began.

I went off to a big football Land Grant University paying a totally reasonable price for tuition and slum housing. I even had a brief stint in prison housing there – they called it an Ag dorm. The only thing good about that prison was meeting the tough inmates who formed our intramural wrestling team. We called ourselves the "*BARBARIAN AGRARIANS.*" We dominated independent team classes and even beat up on the frats for a year or two. We found the only thing that ultimately beat us was beer, itself. You can't make a whole team out of heavyweights.

I got a B.S. degree in Ag., majoring in Agronomy which is basically crop and soil science and a lot of agonizing over classes designed to take more of our money, called "electives." You had to take them to make you "well rounded." We thought they made "well rounded" piles of money for the University. In my last "quarter" I had to clean up some of these electives, and Anthropology 101 almost cost me the job I had already landed. Seriously, I can't remember a thing I didn't learn in that class except for when the reserved Asian teacher lady (who was apparently a closet jokester) handed me my senior final back and said, "David, jou flunked"... well I almost did! All I could see was a $26,000 a year job chock full of benefits flushing down the drain. I barely made it through that class and wonder to this day how one could cram so hard for a test, yet still manage to forget everything!

During those years I was most fortunate to work internships in herbicide research in Ohio, Indiana, Iowa and Illinois. I say fortunate because I do not glow and the internships paid for a lot of my degree, food and housing. Internships also landed me a full-time job while I got to see much of the midwest and further developed a love and appreciation for killing weeds. Herbicides really are a great invention, regardless of the bad name they sometimes get. You go out and take the row of weeds missed by the sprayer with your hoe and a 95 degree sun. Then tell me you don't appreciate this technology!

My first full-time job was selling chemicals to kill weeds and stabilize nitrogen in central Illinois. I then got squeezed into this next great opportunity in the chemical industry called seed corn. Yes, we, the big chemical company, were going to genetically modify corn to resist insects and certain herbicides. I was just a peon and since I had no choice but to be banished to west central Wisconsin Badgerland for this next great opportunity in our industry, I was all in. Six months later those tight old dairy farmers got the best of me and I fired myself, but man they sure were fun to bale hay with! Those Scandahovians had that "work hard, play hard, pray hard" thing figured out. I still miss wearing my Cheddarhead, but it is in good hands now as my brother is farming clear up in Wisconsin against the north woods, badgers, bears, Packer fans and all. Believe it or not, he is also a no-tiller, but on arctic tundra type soils. He is a patient man!

In 1990 I got a chance to further my education while working in extension for the Big Land Grant. Herbicides, one being Atrazine, were coming under fire for showing up in reservoirs and even rain drops, sometimes exceeding the maximum contaminant levels (MCLs) set by industry watchdogs. We looked at techniques farmers could use to reduce the rates and field loss of atrazine and other products while still being able to keep those products around as alternatives. Yes, I did a few years as a bureaucrat, but was lucky enough to work with a boss with a real Doctoral degree, who was very public service oriented and practical.

A year or so into that job I was able to buy my own piece of land for experimentation and a refuge from the city. It was 1991 and land prices were starting to rebound from the '80s farm crisis but the price still allowed for cash flow. It was 83 acres of my own dirt – well, mine and a lending agency called Farm Credit Services. The loan officer gave me the land loan but would not lend me the money to farm it, saying I was cash rich and equity poor, a situation which seems to have reversed itself as I got older and had a family.

I had to go off and seek operating loan money 50 miles away, from a local bank who had loaned me some money in high school. They seemed fine with an operating loan as long as they got paid back, so they took collateral on all the farm equipment I bought. I bought a $3600 Case 930 tractor to start, then a cheap plow, then a disc, then a sprayer and last a $400 old runner style planter. Eventually, I even picked up a $4000 combine with both heads. Might have gotten a good deal on

Dad's old binder truck, but for less than $10,000 in equipment I was farming my own land while also helping a lot of buddies get 30 miles out of a city for their therapeutic "farm fix." That's when I learned the truthfulness of the old adages, "free help isn't always free," and "if you want good help you have to raise it yourself." We had fun, and I'm glad I wasn't involved in raising any of those guys. As soon as I got money ahead, I bought a no-till planter and parked the plow and disc. We all farmed without crop insurance back then, and I always paid my loans back – with interest!

After four or five years that farm just wasn't big enough, so I had to find a mate of the opposite gender to marry so I could afford to purchase more land... and maybe raise some better help! Man did I find an opposite in Jill, at least from the city mouse/country mouse point of view. She was raised under the smokestacks of the Cleveland Ford engine plant and was totally naive as to what life on the farm is like with the bugs and smells and droughts and financial devastation and all. That naive thing came in real handy for a while but she's on to it all now, and somehow we are still married. After some full-time mothering she's back to work as a part-timer in the medical industry where the pay is good, but no benefits, thanks Obamacare. We've had 30 "anniversearies," defined as: an anniversary with your favorite adversary, proof there is a good and gracious God.

We got to looking around Ohio at farms with houses on them so we could house some little Savages and noticed a lot of the land had doubled in value between 1990 to 1995, so we expanded the search to N.E. Iowa where I had worked an internship during college. We stopped in a beautiful town called Luxemburg, it had a handsome church with a tall steeple that looked over everyone's farm as well as the neighboring bar and general store. After having a hamburger at the bar with the mayor, we walked across the road and experienced our first real alive and working general store, post office inside the store and all! There we met a delightful father-son tandem who let us post a note on the post near the farm counter (that might be where post-it-notes came from). On the note was our phone number/

address and that we were looking for a small farm in the area. Eventually, the owner's son sent us a newspaper clipping of a farm he thought we should buy circled in the paper, it was 10 miles away from his store but he could still sell me seed corn and feed! Thanks to his tip of the decade we called the listing realtor and in one weekend that wonderful realtor showed us a half dozen farms that were about a third less cost than Ohio, but otherwise comparable, except the soil was a lot darker in Iowa and being an Agronomist that kind of turns me on. Most of the farms we looked at were older dairy farms, struggling after the extreme weather in 1993. They had lost a lot of hay tonnage and quality due to monsoonal moisture and cloudy weather, and man-made climate change was not even happening yet back in those days, so we had no one but God to blame it on. High hay prices and low milk prices... some were just throwing in the towel. Others had gone into the dairy herd termination/buyout program in the mid-'80s where the government through the USDA basically bought their milk cows for slaughter beef – kind of sad to see those beautiful old barn lots without a dairy cow in them.

Thanks to some divine intervention we landed 186 acres from an awesome retiring couple in a neighborhood of farmers that time hadn't quite changed... and that's a good thing. The picture of that farm is on the cover of this book. We got a glimpse of what farming Utopia, or Agripotia might have been if it ever was, right there in Bankston, Iowa. A place where at one time, the two mile stretch of country road we lived on filled a whole school bus with kids. Almost every one of those farms also had the "mortgage lifter" pigs (until the USDA pig buyout of '98). I suppose there is another whole uplifting story in that farm neighborhood alone, but I'm afraid I couldn't do it justice without a separate book. That formative experience defines Jill and me to this day, and thankfully we get permission to visit many of them and get picked on by their now-adult kids. I can't believe those stubborn and proud farmers of German and Irish descent let us become one with them so fast. At only 186 acres and some beefers, no dairy cows, no pigs, no relatives, we were one of them, and they were fun!

Seven years, almost four kids and four cases of cancer back in the home state later, we thought it best to get closer to our families back in Ohio.

It is not easy to move a farm, but the Iowa crew helped us leave – jokingly I say, we got the hint. We really enjoyed the going away party when they lined up like the ending scene in The Field of Dreams movie, as the group paraded off the hard road down our half mile lane. We had a great time and since the farm had been in the running to be the site for the Field of Dreams movie, it was a "farm appropriate" goodbye. Dad, who taught some Latin, says goodbye is a derivative of God

Bless. I'm good with that, because God blessed us with that experience.

Back in Ohio we had the opportunity to retrace some steps, buy a really good piece of farmland, connect with some old buddies and thanks to one of them we even accidentally got to farm the 83 acre piece I had originally started with, only this time I brought legitimate help Jill and I had raised. Newfound friends and neighbors put up with our goat herd and even tolerated my sisters' two heathen boys who spent many a summer with us specializing in corrupting my perfect children, harassing our yard birds, dogs, six toed cats, and even spying on Romeo the cat-loving runt boar pig. Romeo and his six toed girlfriend cat taught the kids to be open minded, because sometimes nature does throw a curveball! We tried to make our barnyard like one of old, but looking back on it, the road along our front yard kept getting busier and busier, running Fed-ex trucks around the clock. It somewhat limits your freedom and makes you worry about safety and liability, especially with livestock. I try not to be a "worrier" but instead a "warrior," so we started reducing the number of critters.

The scope of our restart farming operation in Ohio started at 200 acres and slowly grew to 900 acres thanks to some family involvement and a good friend who rented me 300 acres for a time. During that growing period I was no longer doing agronomic consulting or custom trucking, so I had to find something regular for a paying job.

The new Ohio operating loan banker was a young guy intent on any "small" farm needing $50,000 of income to cover cost of living – apparently he was taught kids needed new shoes every year. So, I did my rounds at picking up jobs, from working nights throwing packages on a belt at $9.00/hour, to driving a dirt pan for $11.00/hour, and eventually to a job as a crop insurance adjuster, on a per diem deal. All jobs being a means to an end, the end was to get the banker to quit requiring co-signed checks. Every time I would sell a load of grain to an elevator the bank got its name on the check along with mine. After about three years of this unholy relationship I started to distrust my young banker and put the word out that I was looking for a gray-haired banker. Thanks to a local farmer who had been "through it all", I found a great banker who when he lifted his almost gray toupee had no hair left, he had lost it all in the '80s when so many farms were going broke on 20% interest. He reviewed our finances and terminated that over-the-top co-sign stuff, and we did good business together. He lent us reasonable amounts of money and the bank got reasonably rich.

I stuck with the crop insurance job the longest because it had the best flexibility, plus a totally enjoyable group of adjusters to work with. It seems like a lot of them had a school teaching and rural life background. The good lady who recruited me had worked a replant claim on our farm and noticed our barnyard was a little old timey, as in banty hens and road island reds and dogs with multicolored puppies and all. What probably made her think "this guy needs more income" was when a skinny little kid of mine went running across the barnyard chasing a really fast chicken. She asked me what kind it was to be so fast? I said I wasn't really sure; it had come from a buddy named "Heavy" down by the Ohio river (the chicken, not the kid), bordering West-by-God Virginia. She was amazed to hear that the chicken had three legs. "Heavy" told me it was a result of his special breeding program developed because he liked the taste of drumsticks with his taters. When the crop insurance adjuster lady asked me what the drumsticks tasted like, of course I said, "not sure, haven't caught one yet!" Now that's what you call going all the way around the barn to spin a tale.

For the next five years I learned and earned doing crop insurance adjusting and our group saw four different companies in five years. I was not sure why so much change – I never noticed any of our crop insurance companies going broke, just changing nameplates. No doubt working some of those claims helped mold my opinion of crop insurance, but the "lobby" speech probably hit me the hardest. One of the companies had an owner who told us that if we did not give to their crop insurance lobbying group, we should get out. He also put up a very interesting map of indemnity claims which illuminated an obvious problem in claim distribution: it seems certain little areas and the plains states were receiving a disproportionate amount of indemnity money compared to mid-western states. When I asked him about this phenomenon he said, "they are working to adjust rates accordingly," something that has never gotten done. Rates do not reflect risks in crop insurance to the degree they would in any other insurance and that is a problem I will shed more light on.

See the following map of where indemnity payments often appear.

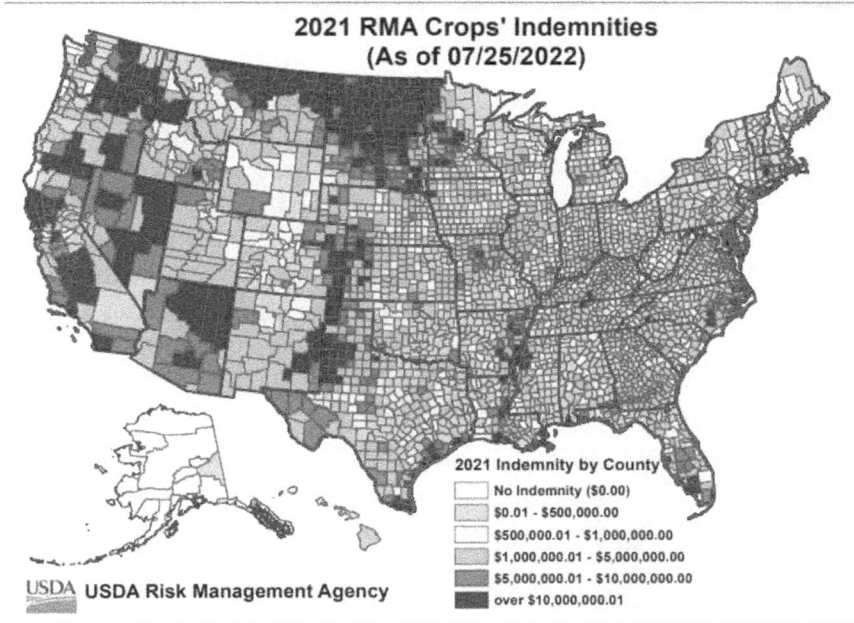

2021 RMA Crops' Indemnities
(As of 07/25/2022)

2021 Indemnity by County
- No Indemnity ($0.00)
- $0.01 - $500,000.00
- $500,000.01 - $1,000,000.00
- $1,000,000.01 - $5,000,000.00
- $5,000,000.01 - $10,000,000.00
- over $10,000,000.01

USDA Risk Management Agency

https://www.rma.usda.gov/-/media/RMA/Maps/Total-Crop-Indemnity-Maps/Crop-Year-2021/072522map.ashx?la=en

Many years of maps show this same phenomenon, where indemnity payments are going to the same areas year after year. It's great for an overproduction philosophy, but basically what's happening is that the midwest is paying premiums to give payments to their "production competition" in the plains states. This isn't my only hang-up with the current crop insurance system. It also didn't help me to see high profile farms rotating "prevent plant" fields around so that they could take the summer months to install field drainage tile, or to see prevent plant used around the famous Ohio flag lots because they were a pain to plant around people's subdivision yards, or hear someone as much as tell you straight out that they weren't going to buy Multiperil crop insurance if they couldn't make it pay out, or seeing an absolute crappy job of slapping a crop into a crappy piece of wildlife management ground and getting a county based t-yield from legitimate farmland to base payments from... all of this being a form of fraud that is hard to prosecute, yet way too commonplace and universal to all areas of this country, even if it is the 5% that are bad eggs. If the government wouldn't subsidize Multiperil crop insurance, companies would price fraudsters out of purchasing it. That's how a free market works; the companies are not stupid.

I soon fired myself from crop insurance adjusting to take on 300 extra rented acres. I also started custom hay work and manure spreading, thanks to the man who found me the banker, the same man who also provided the foundation for the Angus cattle herd I have today. Even though he had been financially torn apart in the farm crisis of the '80s, his attitude toward farming was uplifting, experienced and patient. It took him 30 years to pay off debts incurred in the '80s financial train wreck. He would be the first to tell you he made a lot of mistakes and bad assumptions, but hindsight is 20/20. I think he just farmed at the wrong time and was more specifically at the wrong time in his farming career when the farm crisis hit. So many that age were crushed. Banks too were making bad decisions prior to 1980 with easy money chasing inflating goods like land/buildings/equipment. When the interest rates went skyrocketing, deflation started and at the same time the value of our dollar overseas started going up, hurting exports of our grains, adding insult to injury. Operating loans based on spot interest rates got to 21%. I've been told even non-fixed-rate land loans were unable to lock in rates because rates were changing so fast. How did any business make it through those interest rates? Many Ag banks and farmers did not make it. Hopefully the '80s farm crisis will not repeat itself, but we stand guard. In 2024, interest rates are starting to hurt again, 9% for crop year '24 operating loan. If I borrow a million dollars I'm told I can get it down to 8%, so maybe we are heading for a repeat.

I felt terrible for the farmers and families caught in that brutal period in farm history, but on the flip side of the coin I can say the '80s farm crisis is what paved the way for me to get started in farming. Land and machinery got revalued to something that would allow positive cash flow, and that's back before the crop insurance days. Starting to buy land to farm in the early '90s, I've been in that privileged group of farmers who have never paid more than 11% interest(not saying this is a good rate) and never seen a serious devaluation of land. But I'm bracing up for tough times ahead: we all feel like something has to break as 2024 looks like a year where positive cash flow is hard to find and all costs including land remain high.

After 10 years in Ohio our local public school started a mandatory nanny state drug testing program because... why? Jill and I got caught off guard by this new wrinkle in public education. In 2011, I went to my first school board meeting ever and broke out in hives. I made my case, to the people high up on the stage sitting in positions of awkward silent authority, kind of like those statues on Easter Island but not nearly as endearing. They were like stone-faced robed people, judges that were supposed to be peers, but through their expressionless expressions you could tell they had no time for dissenting opinions. My case was against the nanny state and spending an extra $17,000/yr when the district was already in the red (that means going broke). It seemed to me they already knew the problem kids but wanted a way out for administrators. My argument fell on deaf ears. In other words, I lost, they won. Bureaucrats 2, Dave 0.

Obviously, at the school board meeting I made the mistake of laying down the gauntlet, stating that, "my kids will never urinate in a cup to go to public school." Well, the kids obeyed their dad and promptly got kicked out of every extracurricular activity, including football, driving to school, band, FFA, national honor society, Rotary club, Lodge, Skull-n-Bones society, hanky-panky under the bleachers and all!

Truth be known, I had already gotten them partially kicked out of football because I wasn't taking them to the school 5 days a week all summer to lift weights. They were working on the farm, small square baling, choring 100+ goats, 100 pen pigs, cattle, forking manure, doing firewood, tiling, fencing, defencing, wrenching, picking sweet corn and all kinds of strong back/weak mind farm labor, including building what we think is the world's largest ball of baling wire (not twine). How could they not be in shape? Have you met anyone who dealt with pigs that wasn't strong as a boar? So, when the coach informed my kids they could play, but only on kick-offs and punt returns, I got red in the face and had an early morning weight lifting session with the unsuspecting coach. I lifted away competitively while he declined to lift because of a nagging injury. As jerky as it was for me to just drop in like this, it is also wrong for a public school to exclude the kids who cannot live in that school weight room all summer. A school in the summer is like prison to a farm kid. But as I was reminded, they make the team rules, not me. Once again, I lose... Bureaucrats 3, Dave 0. A big trend has established itself.

What were we going to do? We had decided to make a stand on principle and boxed ourselves into a corner. We had 5 kids to get through high school yet and no desire, patience, or aptitude to do home schooling, especially when already paying 51% of our property taxes to the public school. On homeschooling, it was out of the question because years ago I took a solemn vow to never look at a math problem with letters in it! All the other surrounding schools were doing the same drug testing thing, as drugs have become quite the problem for rural Ohio. Why do we want to raise our kids in that area if drugs are such a problem? My pride is not going to let me surrender to the urine sample thing. As Confucius once said, "Man who stand on own principle, fall on own sword." Well if he didn't say it, he should have.

Within a few months we decided to look around at different farm areas, putting a preference on a thriving cattle industry and schools with no urine sampling protocols. It's a free country. Urine in the barnyard, not in the schoolyard! I was kind of tired of fighting those petty battles and losing; I'd rather lose at bigger battles. We left not really wanting to give it all up in Ohio but hoping to set up a more diversified farm in cow/calf country, a small high school with 6- or 8-man football, less traffic, fewer people, more freedom. Our search began to focus on the cheaper lands and sparsely populated part of southern Iowa.

6.

The Farm Buying Auction in Iowa

Before the land Auction in "Almost Missouri" Iowa we were drawn to a certain area primarily because there was a farm listed in the big Des Moines paper "for sale by owner (FOSBO)". Yeah kids, they used to sell stuff like farms in the classified section of these things that delivered filtered news printed on paper; they called them newspapers. Back before Craig had a list and facecrook took over, they were the big thing. The farm was near a town which had a school with 8-man football. The school graduated with a class size around 20 kids per class, so I felt confident the kids could be in the top 20 even if they couldn't make the football team.

We set up an appointment to see the 320 acre FOSBO farm. It was an awesome farm for the area, but as soon as we pulled up I knew right away we would not be able to buy it. The little flower garden was full of John Deere trinkets, green banners, green bird baths, green spinning things, green flags and green stuff, all with little splashes of yellow. If you're a person of any equipment affiliation other than John Deere's green and yellow, this sight makes your skin crawl. I'm walking up the clean sidewalk trying to hide my Case sweatshirt and Jill already knows our goose is cooked. We are the wrong color, and that is something almost impossible to hide, as this is quite a phenomenon in rural USA. We have mostly red (Case IH) and an older white Case tractor; we already got rid of the ancient calf-poop yellow one. The only way to bridge the tractor color chasm wedged between farm families is to sit in the same church for a lot of years together, on opposite sides of course. Or better yet, go through a tornado together while at church, and have beers afterwards. Anyway, what I'm trying to say is that it takes God's good grace and an altered state of consciousness for Green and Red to get along in farm country. Usually somehow eventually we all figure out how to tolerate one another's paint color preference, all coming to the realization that *we all bleed the same color: RED!* (Got that one off some kids t-shirt at the fair.)

Believe it or not, the folks selling the farm actually asked the qualifying question, "What kind of equipment do you run?" I should have said, "All green – you know what Case stands for: Can't Afford Something Else..." Instead, I was surprisingly honest: "um, mostly red, but I had a John Deere combine once." I left out the part where it caught on fire and the neighbor and I both agreed that I was an idiot for putting it out. Needless to say our offer was not accepted. Later when the local realtor (who was still sore from not getting the listing) heard what we had offered for the farm and what the John Deere guy had rejected, he pulled out the old line, "that's where two fools met." I love those kind of indirect compliments.

While in that area we happened to see a farm with an AUCTION sign on it even closer to town and on a hard road. The farm was 280 acres, going to auction in the fall. This farm must be the one the John Deere guy had said "couldn't raise hell with a fifth full of whiskey." This one had great potential for a guy like me. When I see broken down old buildings, multiflora rose everywhere, gullies and thorny honey locust trees I see a place even a guy like me can help. This farm spoke to me and did not scare Jill too bad, so we thought maybe I should travel back out for the auction.

My dad who was then in his early 80s was game for going out to the auction with me, 670 miles west. He was an awesome road trip companion, very disciplined about his opinions, and while not exactly supportive he was definitely curious and turned out to be a sage voice of reason. The thing that stands out most about our interaction during this trip is that he was very uncomfortable staying in motels/hotels – he always wanted to see if there was a camping option first. I'm worrying about spending a half million dollars here and Dad's worrying about overindulging in a $50/night motel, that he wasn't even going to have to pay for. Seems he missed his calling in life: he was supposed to be a monk and flog himself every day for the original sin event in which Eve talked Adam into eating an apple from the Tree of Life. Even the bunks at Ft. Rucker were not austere enough for Dad.

The auction for the 280 was about to start. There were not as many pickups in the town community hall parking lot as I expected, which seemed strange. We were plenty early and since I had out-of-town plates and stuck out like a sore thumb I had to show some evidence of financial backing. Since I couldn't bring uncle Richey Rockefeller, I decided to bring a letter from my banker instead. At the auction we all sit quietly and I try to figure out where the landowners are sitting and what age group they are in. The auctioneers try to figure out why I'm there since I have not tipped them off and they probably know almost every other player in the room. Dad is in the parking lot, studying readings from the book of Job. I have my calculator ready and the auction is off and running.

After a brief introduction and a final decision by the owners to sell all 280 acres in one parcel, the auction was ready to start. Finally, I get a chance to identify the owners: they are elderly and friendly looking, so my soul was at peace and I could settle in and do my thing. The auctioneer always starts with too high a price and promises you things like, "they aren't making any more land" or "the last one sold for such-and-such," or "the time to buy is when it's for sale," or "you can put it in CRP and let the government make your payments." Anyway, I almost always stay out of the bidding until it slows down, not just because I'm slow, but if you get in too early it sometimes feels like you've been bidding too long and almost get self-conscious about it. The auctioneers were asking mid-2000s/Acre at first but the initial bids came in at less than half and went up in $100 intervals, stalling now and then. I rode out the first couple stalls and finally jumped in around $1600 and got them to take $50/A bids all the way up to $1850 and then the bidding stopped and I was the last bid. I did a quick turn on the calculator to see if I was still OK. Yup, I was OK but they were not, and the gavel did not fall. The auctioneers had a little private pow-wow and decided to take a break. At this point I'm wondering what's up, are they calling my lender? I'm glad I had a seat at the front of the room so I didn't have to watch people watch me squirm. Finally the auctioneers came back and said they made a phone call. The call was to, let's call her "Betty Lou" at let's call it, "the Farmers' most friendly government office (FSA)" where I came to find out she was a loan officer at the time. Seems she had forgotten to put the auction on her calendar and the auctioneer knew she would be interested because she had maybe helped purchase other farms in recent years for her dad, but probably not while on government time. To the auctioneer's credit he announced who he was calling because she was apparently well known in the community.

Now the bidding will commence and I'll have to bid against the phone because she was all in. Up she went to $2000/A and I along for the ride. I hadn't really discussed this kind of price with my financier so I tried a $25/A bump to get her off a round number, they would not accept, so I went to $50/A and the gavel slowly and finally dropped, sold to me for $2050. The phone call made by the realtor cost me $56,000, but look at it on the bright side the realtor/auctioneer made $4,000 more with that one phone call and the sellers got $52,000 more. Poorer Dave.

The auctioneers may have had a moment of guilt as one of them offered to treat us to a steak dinner. I didn't know what to tell him about getting chummy with a guy who just cost me an extra $56,000 – I like steak, but that's an expensive steak! Is any of this really legal or ethical, stopping an auction to phone a friend, buying a personal farm while at your government job, a job which is intended to start new farmers with guaranteed government loans and such? It doesn't really surprise me. Much of the country works this way, where it is not what you know but who you know. I was just getting an expensive lesson in who I didn't really want to know, and the FSA office may not be a friendly place for me. This was really reinforcing my dislike and mistrust of the USDA.

Signing the selling papers started to take some time and I began to worry about Dad. I told the auctioneer I needed to go outside to let Dad know what was going on and that I would not run away. On the way out this brother and sister duo caught me by the arm and said; "we have a farm we want you to look at around the corner from the one you just bought, it's a 240 and it's a better farm," not knowing if that meant, "you just bought a big P.O.S." or what. I flashed back to the disappointing number of vehicles in the parking lot. I told the duo I would be right back and fought off any inclination to run like my buddy Forrest Gump, please stay a few minutes while I check on Dad. This was a lot to dump on Dad all at once, but he had already figured something was up since all the other pickups had left the scene and the only thing left in the parking lot was the Ford Focus station wagon with tent and sleeping bags in it. I asked him if he had any tolerance for looking at another farm, he was stuck there anyway so he was OK with it and went inside to meet the Brother/Sister duo while I finished paperwork on the auctioned farm. We lined up lawyers and I accidentally got a great lawyer from town to help us set up for closing. In the meantime Dad got all the history on the town we were in, and he connected dots on the pilgrimage of religious groups and great western trails he had studied since his childhood. He wasn't much use on figuring out the details on the next piece of land, but it was comforting to see his intrigue about the local history.

The brother/sister duo led us out of town to see their farm. I had the most awful headache and a wrenched gut feeling but sucked it up cause that's what you do when you make your own mess. Anyway, if I was looking for sympathy I wasn't going to get it out of Dad – he's got my old neighbor's attitude: "if you're looking for sympathy, you'll find it in the dictionary between shit and syphilis." The brother/sister duo was correct in the assessment of relative value of their farm mainly because the fences were more complete and land mostly cleared and farmable. The buildings and house in which they were raised had seen better days; they lived in faraway towns now and I think at their age were tired of managing the farm; it's hard to see old memories fade to age and disrepair.

Dad pried a history lesson out of the duo and they proudly laid out the stories of this piece of land and how it tied in with the founding church in the area, how fire had destroyed the proud old barn and how the great depression had burnt them all. I was honored to even get a shot at this farm. By the time we parted I was even convinced Joseph Smith had buried the golden tablets somewhere on that very piece of land! There I go, getting my hopes up. Bonding with the owners did not mean I could swing it, so we left it with an idea on price and my new mission to find a little more financing... well, a lot more financing!

After a pow-wow with a banker who was willing to sign my life away to perpetual debt, I started to deliberate a price with the brother. The back and forth went on for the next two weeks and finally reached a stalemate. It appeared as if someone was privately out-bidding me and I thanked the brother profusely for giving me a shot and hung up the phone and started the rationalization process of how I wasn't deserving anyway, and maybe it was "all in the greater plan" as Mom would say. The greater plan changed the next day as I received a call back from the brother who had compelled his siblings to go with my bid even though it was less than another offer. I believed him about the offers because they were the kind of people who would make a choice of their own free will and instinct. The last dollar might not have been the only motivating factor. I was happy to accept and grateful for the choice they made. I can't help but think they liked the idea of us bringing 5 new kids into the local school. I don't blame them; these little towns need more kids, and these little towns need a school.

A few miracles of lending agencies later and we were heading for a closing on 520 acres of the poorest soil types in the whole state of Iowa. Did I mention lenders are sometimes willing to let you sign your life away and mortgage everything, and the life insurance companies have this relationship to the lender like a sucker fish to a killer whale. Don't get me wrong, I have had great relations with almost all my Ag lenders – without them I would not have gotten a crack at farming. So let's be clear about this relationship, the sucker fish is life insurance, the killer whale is lender, Dave is baitfish.

We still had a problem, however: nothing we bought had an inhabitable house, unless you're a varmint carrying hemorrhagic disease, or rabies/scabies/hairy little babies. We started looking around in town to get a place near the school – after all, it's only 4 or 5 miles to the farms. While searching we caught wind of an 80 acre parcel near our farms. It had a partially finished pole barn on it with a kitchen and an office built into one end. That would be perfect for us, but the money cow had no more milk. I happened to know a sister of mine who was looking for a good investment for some hard-earned money legitimately gained from the sale of a small tech company. Since I helped get her through calculus in high school and also many of her math classes in engineering school with my 3rd grade math abilities, she owed me one and bought the pole barn farm. I was uncomfortable being a tenant to such a hostile landlord so we finally bought her out, and after 7 years of brutal submission to her tyranny we are finally free of her.

All joking aside, whoever said, "thou shalt not go into business ventures with your family" may not have been around the farm business much. In farming the capital outlay for land or equipment is such a big obstacle that many farmers have to work things out with family to have a healthy business. More often than not things work out to the benefit of all involved, but occasionally you end up seeing your neighbor in the news with the bale spears of his loader tractor shoved half way through the in-laws' car... that's when you know at least one party is unhappy.

7.

Moving a Farm and "The Last Conestoga Ride"

It's hard to be a minimalist and be a farmer; unless you are poor. Jill and I were about as minimalist as it gets in farming. During our last move from Ohio to Iowa, while hauling a trailer load of our farm chattel (tanks, tool boxes, spare engines, electric motors, hand tools, hydraulic cylinders, hydraulic jacks, welder, torch, compressor, anvil, work bench, gates, hoses, tires, good parts, spare parts, broken parts, and even parts of parts... etc. etc.) through a neighboring town, a neighbor who unfortunately spotted us made a comment that went something like, "I think Savage was lost, he'd already gone past the junkyard." Really funny, Norm! Had he only known that some of the gates on this load of "junk" were his – inherited, not stolen.

The first move from Ohio to Dubuque Co., Iowa was adventurous, but not intentionally. Since the farm we were buying had tractors but no trucks we decided to sell my old Case tricycle front end tractor to a poor unsuspecting friend who is a mechanical genius, so his competency helped me work through my guilt. We will have to pull the little one ton IH truck with the big cabover Ford F-700 straight truck. This would get two trucks and all the chattel (and appliances) out there in one trip.

We could ride together up front across the prairie in *the last Conestoga*, just like my old wrestling coach had done with his wife, the Pioneer Woman a generation prior. So, there was precedence (but they might have done it in a Lincoln Continental).

Since we had been bumped on our honeymoon flight almost a year earlier, we could use that flight voucher to fly back to Ohio for free, then on the next trip bring both of our regular drivers back out: great plan, aye! What is it they say about the best laid plans of mice and men and how they, "oft fall into a bottle of rye?"

I'll try to make this story more comfortable for you than it was for us. We had to move an apartment and a starter farm from central Ohio to N.E. Iowa with these two old grain trucks. Since I had very little of value, most of the farm stuff could go to the junkyard. So, we used the little truck for farm chattel (stuff), the big truck for households. We threw the final things in the truck load, duct taped the tarp down tight, did a final safety check on the rig confirming good turns/brake/hazard lights/fire extinguisher, then said our goodbyes to Marty and Marianne, dear friends who had helped us load, and had also helped me get Jill to the altar 12 months earlier.

From the start, the trucks were really behaving well together. The custom made hitch from a professional welder was super solid. The back truck had bungee cords shut in the front top of the truck door down to the steering wheel, tensioned just right so it wouldn't sway but would allow for a turn. It followed like a dog in heat. We were really comfortable at 45 mph and confirmed that we could make 55, but why push it? Everything was going peachy until right at the halfway point, about 300 miles into the trip, when suddenly we munched a front wheel bearing on the big truck, and that's exactly what it sounded like: munch.

Luckily we were in my old eastern Illinois Ag chemical sales territory where I had one friend who would still answer my call; thanks, Jim! Actually I can't even remember if we called first as pay phones were the only option and neither one of us had a bag phone (the predecessor to the cell phone). This is a case where you should not curse the fact that you broke down, but rather thank God for the place in which you break down. I limped the rig to his farm. He put us up, ran us around for parts, lent me tools and some great wrenching help: these guys could've rebuilt a tank over the top of a foxhole while taking enemy fire – well, almost that good. Carol packaged some cookies and got us back on the road before the cold front came, and what a cold front it was! How do you repay?

Jim even called some of our other old buddies to witness the rig before we got back on the road, and one of those guys totally honored me by saying, "Savage, if I didn't know you better I'd swear the revenuers were after you." It's ironic he said that, because all of the revenuers were quiet that weekend. We hardly even saw a D.O.T. officer, but they were different back then and probably not as well funded. Do I hear a big "defund the HVE division of DOT?" Please don't defund the snow plow division, I've worked with them and they are awesome. Our motto was, "when the weather sucks, we drive trucks."

So, how do you repay a kind and gracious act like what Jim and Carol did for us? When asked that very question, Jim told me the story of how someone down south helped them work through the breakdown of a truck pulling a horse trailer to a show – it seemed the helping party even lent a vehicle to get them to the show on time. All the helping party asked for in exchange is that the good deed be passed down the line. And that is all Jim and Carol asked of us: pass the good deed along. I too have asked the same of others. I would like to think this is still a common theme in rural American culture. I must admit to having a bias toward helping people who are trying to help themselves, which sometimes takes a while to figure out. In a later story I will illustrate how you can think you are helping one person and end up helping a whole town! See the Red Ford Ranger chapter.

The last Conestoga ride continued. By the time we got to western Illinois, the sky was getting irrationally angry. We were heading into the teeth of a serious cold front, and had a front row seat, in a cabover! This storm ended up dropping sleet first, then freezing rain. Premature darkness was setting in, I noticed my headlights dimming and my wipers slowing. Since I had personally installed this engine taken from a junk school bus, I knew my way around it enough to know that there were many things that could be contributing to a voltage problem, but it was getting too dark to fiddle with it in some parking lot at night, so we found a motel room and we'll deal with it in the morning.

Unfortunately morning came with a click-click-click in the ignition system and light snow cover on the ground. The back truck was a 1970 International Harvester (IH) grain truck with an awesome 304 engine – I was the second generation to get to use this truck on Savage farms – I really liked that truck. No problem, I'll just switch out batteries and try to diagnose the problem in the cabover. The cabover continued to run when I disconnected the battery, which meant the alternator was working and voltage was good, so we started back on our way with the IH truck idling behind to charge up the dead battery.

We were almost to the edge of town, maybe 5 miles, when we smelled burning plastic. Sure enough, we had a fire underneath us in a wiring harness – apparently the wires did not like that much current. I shut the front truck off and we put the fire out quickly, using the D.O.T. approved fully charged fire extinguisher strapped right next to the driver's seat. Now we are in a difficult situation because the hitch is uniquely designed such that the IH was the truck that had to be pulled, so I couldn't just switch them around, and now the front truck is a dead fish. Darn it, I should've had hitch tabs welded to the front truck to be prepared for this eventuality. What's the saying, "hope for the best, but prepare for the worst." Shame on me, but shame is not going to get us delivered to the Iowa farm 200 miles away.

I didn't want to show weakness to my newlywed pioneer woman bride, so I did not cry. I encouraged Jill to look on the bright side, "at least we aren't getting shot at by hostile Illini Indians." As we warmed up our cold fingers in the old IH a brilliant plan came upon my feeble mind: "Since the back truck (IH) is running already, I shall run the electrical system of the front truck with a jump wire connected to the electrical system of the back truck." Of course this plan would involve duct tape and wire (of which I had ample supplies of both because I have a Y chromosome). Since we only had the last third of the trip to go I could afford gassing up two trucks. To this day I am not sure exactly how I accomplished the proper flow of electrons. I'm thinking it was alternator on live fish to the coil on dead fish, or was it connecting coil to coil? Anyway, my first attempt was more successful than I'm used to. I've tried to forget a lot of the specific things I've done in my life, and this is one. All I know is we had to add the electricity way down stream, or else get more fire extinguishers and gas masks. All those episodes of the Red Green Show proved useful, and as he always said, "If the women don't find you handsome, they should at least find you handy!"

After some battery jockeying and frozen fingers we were off to the races. That was on a Sunday and as you might suspect we were driving into seriously cold temps on the back side of the cold front. All the wind particles had "Product of North

Dakota" stamped on them. The thermometer would hit almost 0 F which is cold, but still unbelievably far from a record low for March 1, which is around -20. The guy who engineered our cabover must have been from the equator, because there was almost no heat by design and poor Jill had to wiggle her toes a lot, but she was keeping pretty busy looking for hostile Indians as we crossed the Mississippi into Iowa, leaving Illini country heading into Sioux land, riding shotgun!

This all was not nearly as exciting as it sounds.

Making it to our new farm before dark was not going to be easy, but everything was going pretty well except we were bucking that terrible north-by-northwest wind. Our hopes of making it by dark were suddenly dashed by a fast moving bull rack(semi w/livestock trailer) coming at us, haulin' the mail. He was traveling south bound, we were north bound on a 2 lane state highway. Add his 70 MPH wind vector dragging a gusty 40 mph cold north wind against my 40 MPH non-aerodynamic opposite vector, and bam... he sucked the air right away from my air cleaner... physics sucks! Even worse in reality than it did in high school, as Mr. Hamm (Hemi Hammy) would have loved to ask us to solve this kind of question on a test, I'm thinking the answer would be x=150mph. There I go, I'm not supposed to do a math problem with a letter in it. I'll bet even Hemi-Hammy didn't know the answer to the following question: "How much wind does it take to cause a negative pressure effect in a cabover air intake on a 361 Ford engine fitted to the ugliest truck cab ever made?" Had it been a Hemi motor in a Dodge Super Bee, I'm sure he would know. Seriously, I'd never even heard of that kind of thing happening before – another design flaw of a cabover. Without air, the motor cut out faster than you can say fudge and we had to pull over immediately because we were digging at it pretty hard uphill against that wind, no opportunity to re-bump start with the clutch, wanting to get clear of our lane and onto the wide shoulder. I don't think I could've even found second gear fast enough with the Ford cabover patented 3 foot long "guess-a-gear" manual shift lever, and I wasn't gonna try to bump start it going backwards for fear of that resulting in the ever dreadful jack-knife.

Thankfully Iowa gives a generous shoulder, that's one of the features I have always liked ever since my buddy and I went through Iowa on our highschool road trip/walkabout, we both liked that, and now it's coming in handy. Unfortunately however, this happened right next to a big old grain bin with its bin fan howling in my ear as I had to go through the whole routine of a reboot, tilting the cab up and all. A half hour or so later we were going. After picking my frozen finger tips up and stuffing them back into my Handy Andy's, I had to break the bad news to Jill that making it the last 40 miles with both trucks was not an option. We found an old gas station and parked around back. I left a note on the ugly truck promising them I had not abandoned it, will be back tomorrow, no phone number yet, please give us a day, will gladly pay for the overnight and all. Please, please do not take this load to the salvage yard! Our only chance to sleep at our new farm was to unhook and come back tomorrow on a retrieval mission. Since I was a little concerned about the really cold nights and the condition of the pipes and amount of heating oil at our new old house, we were bound and determined to get to that farm with the old IH. We really appreciated the ample performance of the awesome IH heater; it felt so comfortable as we made our destination finally on the 3rd night. One truck short, mission not yet accomplished.

The next morning Iowa greets us with more snow – like we needed that! We had to hustle because that same night we had tickets to fly out of Cedar Rapids to get our regular driver cars back in Ohio. It was a beautiful morning, that is, if you're tough enough to ignore that bluish/black color in your fingers and toes. We hopped in the old binder (slang word for International Harvester trucks) and headed south on a mission of retrieval. We were still amazed at how quiet the roads were, either we were not calibrated for this part of the world's lack of traffic which is partly true, or this cold front... well, everyone was just flat tired of fighting winter, it's March for heaven's sake!

We got to the old cabover and I was happy to see it was not impounded; no note from the Sheriff to come see him in his office. Had they inspected underneath the duct-taped tarp they would have assumed A.) this guy must be headed for the salvage yard. Or B.) they might have had this sorrowful compassionate response that says, "maybe we shouldn't get involved, what-d-ya think there Barn, Okies or Gypsies?"

Apparently the gas station was not regularly used, or we were too early to find anyone to pay for the overnight parking spot. The reboot went well and the jockeying for a hitch pin position did not cause a divorce. Back on the road with a fresh lease on life, wet roads and a bright sun, everything is good except an ever tightening schedule. Somewhere south of Dyersville, we saw a good omen in the sky: a bald eagle. That big old bird was tracking right in front of us for miles almost as if guiding us home, clear up to New Vienna we kept seeing him. We took it as a sign that the land was blessing us, a token of acceptance and approval, those Illini and Souix weren't shooting at this conestoga, they were spiriting us along. That thought was great to hold onto, for we had been through quite a lot.

Little did we know that bald eagles are very plentiful in Dubuque County, Iowa. They did most of the bird type scavenging that time of year before the buzzards returned from wherever buzzards go in the winter, maybe Florida, with the rest of 'them old Buzzards'. It turns out ignorance is bliss. We came to find out the bald eagles loved foraging through the manure in the corn and soybean fields during the day only to make the 20 mile flight back in the evening to the open fishable pool of water near the Dubuque lock and dam. Of course the eagles always took the longer route; it was only 18 miles as the crow flies.

Does it really matter if it was one or multiple eagle "guides" we thought we were following? I think not. Man, was it ever nice to be within striking distance of our new farm.

There it is, the big red bank barn on the hillside! Same farm view as the cover of this book. Pictures always tend to flatten out landscapes and even as well as our wonderful neighbor painted this picture, it can't do the hilliness justice. As I wrestled that non-power steering cabover wheel into the driveway I could have just dribbled out to my hands and knees to kiss the snow-covered black Iowa dirt, but somehow I had this creeping feeling of dread. I had not yet decided on how we were going to "take the hill" where the house was perched. It wasn't like it would have helped to make a plan to take the hill since every other plan I had made was busted. Was I waiting to see if we would even get to the driveway? Was I waiting to see how much traction my front truck was getting? Was I waiting to see if we could get some speed up without fishtailing? Was I thinking we have 4-wheel drive if I combine two 2-wheel drive trucks, after all the back one is already running anyway? On that last thought, scratch it because Jill was not very good with a manual transmission and that just didn't feel safe. Had it been my brother or dad we would have been 4x4'n that hill for sure. But since discretion is the better part of valor, I just nailed the go pedal, through the flats between the two pole barns, keeping my momentum, Jill yelling encouragement. I'm happy as heck she's not pushing me with the back truck, and up the hill we go digging like a dog on a molehill. The front tires got up on the flat when the back tires finally lost their battle with traction, of course.

I already knew gravity is a "b" and not just a town in western Iowa whose motto is: "WHEN GRAVITY GOES, WE ALL GO" (and if you've ever seen the town, you'd better start booking your reservation). I tried everything short of jumping out and pushing – it was a slow speed descent toward the flats only 150 feet back down my fresh icy tracks. I held the brakes, I dumped the clutch in what I thought was first gear, I prayed two "Hail Marys" and half an "Our Father," I steered to avoid the jackknife until I decided the jackknife is my friend. As I gracelessly slid downhill gaining momentum I could tell I was being sucked toward the very nice modern pole barn... I could picture the headline in the paper with my two trucks stuck through the wall, "Area man proves he can hit the broad side of a barn!" No, first I shall jackknife to save my bride and my pride. As painful as it was, I went with the jackknife, or did it go with me, and we finally slid to a grinding halt, perhaps executing the first ever successful jackknife. Some metal got bent, but mainly only in the hitch pin. We were safe, the pole barn was safe, the trucks needed to be shut down and I had to go clean out my britches. As you often hear when luck is on your side, "at least no one got hurt."

Many of you are asking yourself, why not first unhook the two trucks and take them up one at a time? In a normal world of two functioning trucks I believe that to have been the prudent option, but in our world the back truck was needed to run the front truck, so they kind of had to be delivered as a package and that package had to get to the top with all our furniture and kitchen stuff and clothes, etc. We had a lot of work ahead of us and not much for time.

The whole adrenaline thing was barely starting to leave our bodies as we began to assess just how we would proceed from there, all the while thanking our lucky stars to even be where we were. It turns out the neighbors weren't going to let us fail. Before I even got a chance to decide what to do next, we look up to see a Jeep coming down our ½ mile lane and since there would not be time to hide our embarrassing wreck we decided to act cool and embrace it. In the Jeep are probably the new neighbors who live right across from the end of our lane, and they probably witnessed the whole thing. I can only imagine what was going through their minds when they pulled up and confirmed the Beverly Hillbillyishness of the whole contraption. We had no idea if they would be mad at us for buying a farm right out from under them, or paying too much for land, or maybe they were going to let us know right away that our half of the fence needed rebuilding, or maybe the last owner still owed them for hay or any number of things. Instead of all these worries the smiles and greetings and warmth they immediately shared lifted our spirits and gave us a dose of renewed energy.

You could tell this husband and wife worked as a team. They were tough, hard working, fun loving people. Fun enough that Richard eventually got tagged with the endearing nickname of "the Dick at the end of the lane." Our friend Dogkiller, a bin buster (who got his nickname from a motorcycle accident involving an unfortunate dog) was responsible for tagging him with that name. Dick has graciously embraced it clear up to his 80th birthday party. Back to our jackknife situation, within minutes the two of them, Dick and Carol, decided to go grab one of their many tractors and pull our truck to the top of the lane. I got a hammer and hacksaw, unhooked the back truck and a few minutes later was tickled to see an awesome John Deere 4020 slow and steady coming down the lane (probably in road gear Betty!) fully outfitted with tire chains, loader, heat houser and all. With ease, Dick pulled me up the hill, and our life of being in debt to all the Bankston area neighbors began.

That neighborhood could have a book written about the dynamics, the history, the churches, the welders, the pig men, the dairymen, the beautiful barns, and the military trails (you go, Jack and Maria). The delicate balance of working with others but doing for yourself was negotiated about as well as can be done. If I were pressed to identify the components of that farm community that worked like cogs in a gear, I would put: God, family, work, church, community, welder, card club, beers, sense of humor, and welder. I mention welder twice because they often helped get us through the down times, sometimes as machinists, sometimes as therapists. Many in that community were content to farm just their own piece of land, often less than 300A, but to do this they all had a livestock enterprise. You might say at least a remnant of Agritopia existed there. Unfortunately, during the 7 years we were there we witnessed the small and moderate sized livestock operations begin to go away, CRP came in and indirectly raised all the rents, and as the pigs and the dairy left, the competition for more acres per farm began. It's hard for any community to stay together with all that pressure to compete, but Bankston does a pretty good job....even without a bar!

Continuity of church affiliation has always seemed to help Ag communities; I noticed this in Wisconsin also with the Lutherans. Sayings like "we're all in this together" and "love thy neighbor" do rub off. We had a set of jovial land neighbors who had an awesome dairy farm with red tractors and a beautiful yellow Case 730 tractor (later used as the model for a big ⅛ scale model toy). They joked with us about how to interpret broken barbed wire on the line fence between our farms: if the top wire was broken, it meant the bull was on the loose and your cow might have a calf that looks like a Holstein(dairy breed). If the bottom wire was cut, you might end up with a kid that looks like a sneaky dairy farmer. I don't think that was the correct application of the principle "love thy neighbor!" Of course I'm just having fun here with an urban legend from rural America... I think!

Since reliving the story of this move to N.E. Iowa wears me out, I will vastly abbreviate the story about moving back to Ohio 7 years later. The move was less traumatic – we cheated, because by then we had a semi-tractor and a friend with a semi-tractor and drop deck trailer. All the household items fit in my hopper bottom grain trailer, and most of the farm equipment fit on a drop deck, owned and operated by the best husband/wife farm pond blue-gill fishermen in Iowa, speaking of characters. He recently sold his semi so he is now declaring himself,"semi-retired." I might add, there is a fisherman who came before them that is better.

The last farm move back west to almost Missouri Iowa 10 years later did have a twist. The semi was still being used to farm in Ohio, so pickups had to do the bulk of the work. We moved at the break of school around Christmas so we could get the kids enrolled in the new semester. The cabover and the binder were gone; Jill was very disappointed with that! Many opportunities to get another load awaited us since we were kind of setting up a western headquarters, not knowing what to expect, but going back and forth a lot. The winter gave us the opportunity to modify an existing structure inside a pole barn to what one may refer to as a house. We treated it like we were homesteading and had to "prove out" before next winter – a pretty wimpy version of proving out when you have electricity and running water and indoor plumbing. Eventually, the trusty old Case 1070 tractor and a bulldozer showed up on a bought-and-paid for drop deck trailer load. Talk about feeling naked and vulnerable: I went 3 months without my Case tractor, in fact, no tractor at all! That load cost me dearly, at nearly $3000 and it was not a wide load. The next equipment I had to get out here would take three wide loads, up to $5,000 a crack, and that would have added up to a lot of money in trucking.

Since I have some Irish in me, I found it necessary to come up with a cheaper plan. So obviously the only thing to do was drive my two big tractors pulling the wide equipment west, as I needed them. It would be 670 miles or so for each tractor using the good old two lane state and federal highways of the midwest. With 18 and 20 mph speeds the trips were slow but pretty routine and inexpensive. I'll tell that tale toward the end of the book.

Case 7220 w/ auger cart and manure spreader.

I think our days of moving farms is over. Short of the Yellowstone Caldera blowing its top and covering our farmland in 10 foot of ash, we're done now. I don't think we are young enough to do it again.

That's what it takes to move a farm.

8.

Pigs Have Left the Area!
How Government Intervention of
the Last Few Decades Changed
Midwest Farms.

Before I further eviscerate government involvement in farming, here is my disclaimer: as I have mentioned before, if you are a farmer, you probably should be in these government programs to compete and to keep a banker! The system is set up so that you cannot operate in a bubble without some other radically different economic situation, like maybe your great uncle was named Rockefeller, or maybe because you are extremely "committed" (hopefully not to the nuthouse).

In N.E. Iowa ('95 to '02) the young folks were not coming back to those farms like previous generations had. A lot of this had to do with the vanishing of "the mortgage lifter" pig, or should I say the reallotment/redistribution of the pig to larger confinement operations consolidating ownership and production. Prior to 1997 a lot of pigs were still being raised in outdoor or at least indoor/outdoor pens, many over slats, some on straight concrete, and a few on dirt. 5 out of 6 Iowa pig farms left the industry in the 25 years prior to 2002. When we were there in the late '90s, the buying stations were shuttering, sale barns disappearing and options for selling pigs in the open market were vanishing. In 1998 the price for piglets got so low that farmers going to a sale barn in the area had to put a lock on the doors of the livestock trailer to avoid getting filled with "free" piglets. I'm recalling stories of $8/cwt going around, that's around $20 for a finished pig. I did not know how farmers were surviving because most of the corn was walking off the farm on pigs' feet; I suppose most were just burning equity.

Simultaneously a disease came along called pseudorabies which is often fatal especially to young piglets, and along with that disease came a government program to buy out infected herds and push for eradication of the disease in domestic swine herds. First, your herd had to test positive for the disease; this did not seem to be a problem for most herds in the area, as it was very transmissible and the government was paying 3 times the market price for pigs from an infected herd. I'm thinking economic incentive and transmissibility were somehow connected, if you know what I mean.

It was a sad sight to see: government veterinarians in white Tyvek suits walking around a barnyard like Martians, euthanizing barrels full of piglets, with semi-trucks lined up along the road to carry every larger pig off the farm. Not only were we witnessing the end of an individual farm's pig legacy, we were witnessing the end of the independent pig farmer: bye-bye mortgage lifter, hastening the end of the middle class farm. Was the government buyout/pseudorabies eradication program causation or correlation?

To farmers it looks more like causation. The word on the street (or gravels) was that the buyout program existed to get the rest of the small guys out of the way so the big integrators could take over. If there is such a thing as collective wisdom I think they were right: now most of the pigs in Iowa and the U.S. are owned by vertical integrators who use cheap labor to do the chores for pigs owned by the integrator, often in buildings owned by the farmer with lease back agreements with the integrator. The waste product, manure, is a liability to the integrator, as is the building depreciation and wear and tear. The manure is often turned into an asset by the farmer, but the building is pretty much a single-purpose structure. Unlike the cattle business, almost no one is left in the pork business marketing pigs independently through traditional sale barns or buying stations. We call this being "chickenized," since the poultry industry paved the way for this kind of vertical integration model.

Big picture question: did Psuedorabies even need a pig buyout program, as there was testing and vaccines available which ended up being the ultimate means to eradication? Here, USDA buyout programs were involved in reshaping an industry. Is this how they model the way "they" want an industry to operate? How much different would our industry be without that intervention is a question we cannot answer.

In 1986 there was a dairy herd buyout and many farmers submitted a bid and eventually won the lottery, and the cows left the farm. Enough of them went to slaughter that the beef market hit the skids by 25%. So beef cattlemen took that one in the shorts because dairy "cull cows" entered the beef market at least for a time. In the long run, however, the dairy buyout seemed to accelerate the consolidation of the dairy industry to fewer farmers, fewer processors and now mega diaries milking thousands of cows per operation with multiple lagoons, backed by a new government subsidized insurance system that helps with economic sustainability. Sarcastically I say, at least you should feel good that they all have a manure management plan... and, the Chamber of Commerce and Farm Bureau will make sure they have documents for their workers. After seeing a farm show report on the American Farm Bureau convention held in Las Vegas Jan. 2024, with their emphasis on getting more guest workers, calling labor, "the biggest problem facing agriculture." Looks like they are willing to throw all "non-guest worker" farms into the ash heap of history.

Where was that economic sustainability plan when we had a bunch of mid-sized dairies using family labor? It wasn't there, but a buyout was. Not a bailout, but a buyout. Now it's the other way around: we give large scale farms a bailout (examples, Covid relief CFAP 1&2, PPPs, production insurance) and not a buyout. It's much like the Feds bailing out big banks and letting the small ones fail. Anyone who says, "kids just didn't want to go back to those dairy farms" does not know the farm culture of Wisconsin and northeast Iowa. So many of those kids wanted to milk cows, but $12 milk was not going to allow it. I don't think the mega dairy concept has helped the consumer price for milk, butter, or cheese.

Are you seeing a trend yet? Government (USDA) leverages an era of low prices to design a program that messes with normal economics on the farm, always paved with good intentions, which accelerates the trend toward industry consolidation, more corporate farms, and fewer independent proprietor farms. Since bigger farms mean bigger risk we now have the taxpayer subsidize an insurance system because the cost of failure is too high. I maintain that the free market would have kept many more individuals on mid-sized pig and dairy farms, and had you given them an option like my proposed HFSA, there wouldn't even be the need for subsidies. Government (USDA) intervention changed those industries to the detriment of rural America. Maybe the transition to mega size everything is inevitable even in a free market, but we will never know in agriculture because the USDA is always out here messing with our economy. Could we be any worse off had they stayed out of it? We still receive low prices for our overproduced commodities anyway; corn is now (2/24) trading 20% below the cost of production.

Simply put, more competitors are better and get us closer to capitalism, fewer competitors are worse and push us toward socialism. What we have in Agriculture now is a hybrid between capitalism and socialism, you might call it a "distortalism" defined in Dave's Dictionary as, "a system where government designs successful business models based on subsidies and regulations, distorting the outcome away from a meritorious capitalism toward an egalitarian socialism, doing all while refraining from public ownership (except in Western lands and water)."

A concerning trend in the Midwest is to see mega farms relying on illegal alien labor/guest worker programs, first done in truck crops, next in poultry/pigs and dairy, now coming to a grain farm near you. As a proprietor who relies on my own self and family for labor by design, **cheap labor is my competition.** I wish they would stop the influx of illegals at our borders, for many reasons, only one of which is labor. In December 2023 Reuters news service reports 300,000 illegals crossed into the USA, in one month alone! That's pretty close to 10,000 per day. That's an invasion, quite literally it could be. Unbelievable! If you get your news from a cell phone, you may not know any of this, please find yourself an AM radio. If this is an invasion, I'm glad rural USA is home to a lot of great military veterans, as many of them return to their roots. It was reported in and around 2010 that 44% of army recruits came from a rural zip code area representing only 17% of U.S. population. Welcome Vets!

If these new cheap laborers were all destined to replace white collar college educated, privileged class workers, I'll bet the border wall would be built and enforced with ample numbers of border security agents in a hurry. I have no sympathy for agribusinesses who can't find labor, that is if they are designed to exploit cheap illegal labor. As I said earlier, the Farm Bureau and the Chamber of Commerce Republicans, and the Democrat party want this cheap labor, while many of us in our farming communities do not.

9.

Stories About My Competition in the Labor Market

About midway through the 10 years we were at the Ohio farm, some mega dairy farms got started right in our neighborhood, ironically started by mostly Dutch dairymen with temporary visas. I guess the Dutch dairy farm model was an environmental challenge for their country, so they came to the USA to challenge the groundwater here too. The Ohio Department of Agriculture (ODA) even came to a local meeting promoting these new dairies, saying they would all have manure management plans, impeccably engineered lagoons, top management and be able to buy crops from area grain farms in exchange for manure. The ODA was concerned that without these dairies we would no longer have a dairy industry in the state, because dairy farm families were so busy, "they couldn't even get to their kids soccer games." My buddy and I were really bothered by that assertion, as he said, "soccer isn't even an American sport!" Maybe he should have said, "not a United States of America sport." I think 600 cows was the original design but everyone knew that was just the starting point – now one milks 1000 or more. These are the type of farms modeled around a cheap/transient/plentiful supply of labor, legal or illegal, I don't think it matters.

When dealing with one of these dairies, they asked me about organic crops since I have had some experience in doing that production practice, I warned him that weeds are an absolute killer to organic crops and manure carries a bunch of weeds. He would have to rotary hoe twice and cultivate three times because of course there are no miracle herbicides allowed. I said, "that's 5 extra trips after 2 to 3 trips to work it down, a lot of fuel, time and labor." He said in reply, "nothing there $7.00/ hr can't do." Minimum wage was $6.55 in 2008. Proving their model is built entirely on the backs of cheap plentiful labor.

We were growing sweet corn at that time to sell at a self-serve "honor system" stand down by the gas station. I had been doing it for a few years and successfully so. Being a trusting fellow we had a chicken waterer labeled, "Please pay here" and around the hole at the top we wrote "in God we trust." The system worked well, customers would count out their own dozen or even baker's dozen, multiply by my posted price per dozen and even open up the chicken waterer to make change. I knew how much corn I put out in the morning, counted my modest cash at night and was always close. That is the only way I would sell sweet corn, and I loved it.

Loved it until my sweet corn supply started disappearing without the cash appearing. One night the money count came in a little on the light side; that doesn't seem right, maybe I didn't count the dozens correctly. The next day I really did a thorough inventory and money tally....not good. The third day they cleaned me out, but in their defense they did not take the dollar bills I would leave in the bottom of the chicken waterer, to make change. That ended my sweet corn selling days.

Who was taking my sweet corn? The main suspects were the new laborers showing up to milk cows at the new dairy. There is no way they could know our rural culture, the honor system, or even our language. I must give the benefit of the doubt to language as the primary problem. If I change the instructions to Spanish will I stop the sweet corn from vanishing without payola? I gave up on that idea real quick because the only word I remember from hillbilly dialect Spanish class in high school was cerveza, which means beer, I think. I know correlation does not equal causation, but put yourself in my shoes and tell me if you would run a not-for-profit sweet corn stand to the benefit of those who might take your job next. I am not Saint Isidore (patron saint of farmers), but I wouldn't mind having a cerveza or two with him, followed by a warm feast of chile relleno peppers/refried beans/rice and for dessert, tamales. Food brings us all together, just not free sweet corn!

Language is a barrier I don't know how these big farms are dealing with. One day I found a compact car parked right in the middle of an iced over back road just outside the mega dairy farm lane. I carefully pulled to the side and could barely see a figure in the car for all the ice and fog on the windshield and windows. I thought, why would anyone stop to "make out" right in the middle of the road, so I figured instead this person was having trouble. A knock on the door and the fellow finally opened it, no girlfriend. While asking him what the problem was, I slowly figured this guy doesn't know a lick of englesimo. Believe it or not the poor fellow had driven about a half mile from the barn with about a quarter inch of ice still pasted everywhere on his car and yet he still didn't have the defroster on, not even the fan. Since I was very familiar with his Grand-am, because mine was still parked behind the barn hiding from the salvage yard, I taught him what the positions of his car fan and heater/defroster controls did. We bonded a little bit, smiling over the fan that blew heat, yea! No words to communicate, just grunts, hand signals and a smile. I took my time scraping his windows, and hope I left him my scraper, but can't remember. After admiring how nice his Grand-am still looked, it must have been a Texas car, mine was a Cleveland car with rust holes big enough to stick your head through and wiggle your ears, eventually I drove off ahead of him slowly so he would get the point that the road was very treacherous, hoping neither one of us would meet a milk tanker on that narrow township road with absolutely no shoulder.

What do you make of all this? How far out in a different land did this person come from to not know what a car defroster does? If he was that sheltered from modernization, why would he have ever left in the first place. Wouldn't home be better than getting shit on by a Holstein in the middle of the night? To not know a lick of English. To be unable to read a single road sign. How did he get a driver's license? How safe can this be for anyone? How in the world is it all going to work? How can I find a car this rust free?

Don't even tell me legal Americans won't work. I've worked a bunch of crap jobs, right there side by side with some darned good hard working USA laborers. For instance, the big city landfill, in the mud, the methane smell of garbage 10 hrs a day, risk of stepping on a druggy's needle, fighting darkness and broken equipment, wondering how some of these guys working next to me have done this for 10 or 20 years? What would motivate any person to get there at 4:30 in the morning, in the dark, pouring down rain, open the gates, fire up his 30,000 hour beast of a machine and do the same thing he did yesterday just hoping for fewer problems than he had the day before? It's called pay and benefits (and a good boss sure helps!) I can't help but think that if a job isn't worth a respectable wage, it's not a necessary job. If you're having trouble getting workers, try paying them!

Also, in that "don't even tell me department." Don't even tell me the cost of food will go way up. As a country, we are guilty of wasting 30-40% of food. I should know – I never had to pack a lunch when I worked at the landfill. I see our local Amish families who have worked hard to establish a very good marketplace for truck (buggy) crops, using family labor I might add. Beautiful quality crops: tomatoes (greenhouse and field), asparagus, beats, beans, broccoli, cabbage, cucumbers, melons, onions, squash, watermelon, and zucchini (If my favorite cow named Zucchini doesn't get to these first). At times during the season they will almost have to give away any one or many of those listed crops. Ironically, the very crop humans don't eat much, pumpkins, sell for big money for months in the fall. White pumpkins, warty pumpkins, green/yellow/ red/orange mottled peanut pumpkins, big pumpkins, little pumpkins even those evil orange pumpkins, they all sell well, why? Because they are recreational and not food. Apparently food is too cheap if we can throw out 37% of it.

For the sake of argument, let's say there is no existing pool of cheap labor for mega farms to tap into. First thing they will need is to evaluate how much capacity they can hold onto with additional investment in technology managed by fewer and more highly paid laborers or family. Let's say this labor situation results in fewer barns full of pigs, fewer cows milked, or fewer acres farmed. Good for the rest of us who are competing for the same land, or cows, or shackle space. Maybe this opens up an opportunity for a young farm family working as a subcontractor on his own time to save that mega farm from doing it in house. Having more people with a sense of ownership and being involved in the farming business is a good thing and would be the ultimate result from the loss of illegal or cheap labor. It looks like a lot of people might have to find a new jobs as A.I. comes along and replaces jobs like customer service reps (wonder if A.I. will fake an unintelligible foreign accent just to make help centers seem authentic), receptionists, human resource reps, market analysts, writers and so many more. I think the only business A.I. can't replace is the oldest business in the world, if you know what I mean. Maybe a deindustrialization is ahead, where agricultural production jobs and "re-habitation" of rural America becomes necessary just for employment.

10.

Back to Pig Farms

The pig farmers were caught in, "play the game or get slayed." Everyone knew it was now going to be "get big or get out," which meant big investment in new structures, new pits, lagoons, etc. Now you get to the other side of the bank. The mortgage lifters were now the mortgage creators or at least the building loan creators, somehow I think this worked out well for that J.P. Morgan Uncle.

One of the biggest disappointments to me was seeing the USDA NRCS office trying to be relevant by busting down on the mid-sized livestock farms in the N.E. Iowa area for any violation they could find regarding manure. It's kind of like that Stalin era motto, "show me a man and I'll show you his crime". It seemed they were eager to get every mid-sized guy out, so they could have control of the farm via a "Manure Management Plan," a bureaucrat's dream accumulation of paperwork all based on theoretical assumptions, long on good intentions and short on performance. 25 years and thousands of these "plans" later, you need only look at the current water quality problems in many midwest cities and lakes and the Gulf of Mexico to realize that performance in terms of water quality is lacking. Yet in our farm press you would think we have clear streams, no black snow, and mermaids bathing in our wetlands. That's their story and they're sticking to it.

On Jan. 22, '24 the AP (Associated Press) reports that the EPA's newly released numbers from 2018-19 sampling showed a little improvement in phosphorus pollution and no improvement in nitrogen pollution for rivers and streams contributing water to the Gulf. I gave up trying to find the exact date of their last study, but I think this study is conducted every 3 years and includes bad news for snails, beetles, worms and bottom dwellers as well as species diversity in fish. Looking at some of the EPA long term water quality graphs it seems we started having Nitrogen and Phosphorus problems around 1980 and haven't corrected it in 40 years, and I would agree this is not a 100% agriculture problem, but 90% wouldn't surprise me.The EPA's hypoxia task force has been working on this nutrient loading problem since the late '90s, about as long as manure "mismanagement" plans have been around, with very little progress.

There are a few problems with the Manure Management plan area. Sarcastically I say, "No one would ever pull a baseline soil sample for one of these dung documents out of a fence line which has never seen fertilizer or manure, or would they?" How about a field that tests low enough to qualify for a liquid application but the tractor jockey was unaware of a surface tile inlet, French drain, terrace basin inlet, or as is most often the case, a broken subsurface tile with resulting suck hole. A manure management plan would never approve an application rate of 7000 gal./A while ignoring the turn of a drag line which is slow and awkward and dumps maybe 3 times more on an area which is often near a waterway or creek, or would it? I've seen it: within minutes of a drag line application, run by a very conscientious owner/operator, at the turn near a subsurface field drainage tile, where the injection knives had to be lifted to make the turn, manure began flowing out tile outlets. Hurry up and plug the tiles with inflatable football bladders. If you're not managing the drag line application like a hawk, tiles provide a direct conduit to the creek; sometimes this results in low dissolved oxygen levels and associated fish kills. No-till with worm holes and soils that percolate well actually make this problem worse. Pollution does not always happen with this system, but this

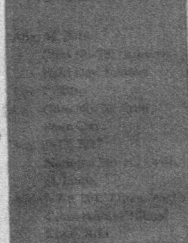

Water quality advocates say voluntary actions not working

Billions Spent; Is Soil Healthier Today?

$77 Million for Lake Erie

dragline system is the single highest environmental risk of any agronomic practice I've ever seen. Unfortunately, I know this all from firsthand experience and cannot ignore that it happens more than we want to think. Since I have personally never seen an environmental/pollution problem with the manure when it is being tanked, that has become my personal preference, despite soil compaction issues. Experience taught me that the beneficial microbiology carried in the manure compensates at least partially for the negative effects of soil compaction.

I have also experienced the environmental issues of our "manure management plan era" from the other end of it, as a dad who wanted to take my kids swimming at the public lake, only to find the beach closed for toxic algae blooms. For rural kids these lakes are an important place to learn to swim and learn to tolerate total strangers who may throw sand in their face. Rural lake beaches introduce kids to other cultures as it is often a great melting pot, especially for those who cannot afford swimming pools or are not fortunate enough to live in that van down by the river rope swing. Too often these lakes are shut down and it seems to be getting worse, and yes the geese are a problem too. You'd be a fool to drive out of your way without first checking postings for water quality alerts and swimability/fishability warnings. If we are going to be cheerleaders for our Ag industry we'd better start getting some of this stuff straightened out; it's almost as if we are not allowed to have a conversation about this problem. I argue that going to large-scale confined livestock was the "wrong turn in Albuquerque," at least in terms of pollution. If you stretch that thought out even farther and look at Chinese ownership of these large scale livestock industries, why do we allow China to take a dump in our own backyard, metaphorically speaking of course.

How many 400 bushel sized manure spreaders, or 4000 gal. liquid tankers (honey wagons, like those used by the mid-size farms), even if they were dumped directly in the stream, would it take to kill fish for miles? It would take dozens of farms contributing intentionally carelessly at 4000 gal. a crack, but it takes only one screw up of a big liquid dragline. The problem has now become, how are you going to tank enough liquid to empty a million gallon lagoon in the short fall and spring windows between crops? It's too big for tanks: it would be 250 turns at 4000 gal./load. Not to mention there may be multiple lagoons per location. My point is that we have gone backwards environmentally by consolidating and regulating. And yes, I think the government is guilty of precipitating this environmental problem, because they were at least complicit in ushering many mid-sized operations out the door with "advantage big" policies.

I've not seen any system that can totally avoid some pollution. A lesson at the big U taught, "the solution to pollution is dilution." The most ideal systems will only be able to limit but not eliminate nutrients lost. I spent a lot of time in the late '90s pulling late spring nitrate soil samples for those mid-sized farms in northeast Iowa. I was lucky enough to work with a really conscientious group of farmers affectionately known as "The Bin Busters," mostly corn/pig and corn/alfalfa/dairy farmers who were attempting to put a number on the value of their manure for fertilizer, trying to figure out if a manure application provided sufficient nitrogen, or if we would need to sidedress additional Nitrogen on the corn crop. They were trying to get it right, and I was trying to make a living while helping them. We found many opportunities to totally cut out purchased inputs of commercial fertilizer, and often found it necessary to use only a little nitrogen up front to prime the pump until soils warmed enough to mineralize manure applied nutrients. Often we found a lifetime of phosphorus (P) residing in their soils and sometimes almost a lifetime of potassium (K), two of the very necessary plant elements in that bag of fertilizer that has an N-P-K analysis on it. To them manure was an asset, not a liability, a situation which reverses itself as livestock operations get too big.

While the pork industry has been consolidating, the U.S. farmers' share of the consumer dollar in pork has slipped to 18% with 95+% of pigs now under either ownership or a contractual agreement with a packer, with a whole lot of Chinese ownership along the way. Poultry got there before pigs, and beef is heading that way, unless we can stop it. Now you know why I write so much about beef in this book....the mid-sized farms and ranches have to hold onto at least one low investment, mortgage lifter type livestock entity, so we fight for cows.

Many of the former mid-sized pork and mid-sized dairy farms that wanted to still have livestock have transitioned to Cow/calf operations, looking for cash flow, seeking to stay independent of a big integrator, also trying to avoid big investment in facilities.

A lot of this comes down to access to markets for the independent farmer and rancher. We still have some livestock sale barns dotting the countryside, pulling together sales of feeder calves and backgrounded calves and beef cows for breeding or cull. It is still a thing, but seems like a fleeting thing and as a guy in our beef group put it the other day, "these sale barns need to join our group, because they're on the *Do Not Resuscitate List.*"

The loss of independent livestock really hurts small town USA. Kind of like that motto for the town of Gravity, Iowa, "if Gravity goes, we all go." When the independent markets go, we all go. I know this firsthand: when our local hog buying station in Ohio closed, my next choice was a marginal market 50 miles away; that's when I started to transition to Cow/calf. The question in my mind: is there a future for "product of USA" beef, or can foreign owned packers transition enough South American rainforest into grazing land to put the U.S. cow/calf industry out of business?

11.

More on Beef

I just got the Cow/Calf breakeven numbers for 2023 from a beef extension specialist, and no it was not Hank Kimball from the Green Acres T.V. show either. $1586 for a Cow/Calf pair according to one of the USDA's most trusted research arms and $1520 according to a non-USDA source, so let's round it down to $1500 to keep a cow all year. A cow who in turn yields a 500 pound "feeder calf," if all goes well. Jill and I currently have a moderate sized cow/calf operation to complement our grain/hay/timber/custom work/WPA/WFFP farm. Ours is an average sized beef operation, bouncing between 40 to 60 head of mommas. Last I checked, average cow herd size was still in the 40's. We will sometimes take that 5 weight calf, wean it from momma cow, get it accustomed to a feed bunk and take it up to 700 pounds, this is called "backgrounding" which is the second stage of the beef making process. The third and final stage is "finishing," where a feedlot feeds a finishing ration which will take that steer or heifer to 1300-1500 pounds live weight, putting some really good tasting protein right under the hide.

For my part in this process I rely almost strictly on pasture, corn stalks, cover crops and cheap round bales of grass hay to get that cow/calf pair to the point where I wean a 500 pound calf, no grain needed until after weaning for us, unless it gets cheaper than hay, which it has been in 2023/2024. This year (early '23) that calf brought $1000. Yes, your math is correct, that's a $500/head loss according to the pro analyst. Almost $500 of this cost is labor and depreciation which ranchers have been "giving away" for years. The extension guy who found these numbers for me was astonished that the cow/calf costs were so high, I can't say I was surprised. Sometimes you accidentally educate the educators. I've always questioned my sanity with this cow herd. I've tried backgrounding and years ago finishing. My current land use fits cow/calf best. I like cows but not enough to run a not-for-profit entity and just like the rest of farmers and ranchers, I'm thinking I can do it cheaper than the next, wood gates, baling twine and all. With land values and real estate taxes where they are, the exodus from the cow/calf sector will continue unless we get paid more for the calf. The profit made by everyone else in the beef business is predicated on the losses incurred by the cow/calf sector. Now, I must say in 2024 our late February sale of feeder calves was profitable, the first time since 2014 (lending credence to that fabled 10 year cattle cycle). Yippie! Grains on the other hand are trying to make sure to get rid of any excess income.

Once upon a time the N.E. Iowa Bankston area farmers tried to teach me this lesson which somewhere along the way finally stuck with me. They would say that is why they diversified, so that when livestock was down maybe grains would be up and vice-versa. From the 90's to today the Land Grant economists have been telling us to specialize in something as they design an insurance system (on the backs of taxpayers) to smooth out the risk of non-diversification. Now you see why a guy like me who does not have a big insurance subsidy and all the other USDA payments must diversify, and must fight for an independent beef system.

One might ask, why not take your calves all the way to a finished product. I did that for a time. I would go to a sale barn 50 miles away, one that was still in the business of buying "fats." When you only take a few at a time, there was always a reason for being 10 to 20 cents below the "market." On a 1400 lb. steer, that equals $140 to $280 under the market, pretty ugly when the average margin is probably $100/hd. on the finishing end. I call that, getting beat up. Some people call that, getting screwed. Whatever you want to call it, it ended my "era of donations to the packer buyers." So now, the only bovines I fatten for slaughter are for freezer beef where I can keep the hormone implants and medicated feed out of them and self-determine the selling price to some extent.

12.

Finishing Wild Cattle

Another experience I had with fattening cattle about 30 years ago came early in our farming experience. The plan was to put together a group of heifers, uniformity of size and 40 in number was important because it would be enough to fill a "cattle pot" or "bull rack," which is country slang for a semi-load of cattle. I went to the bank first of course and laid out my plan to buy 5 weight heifers, background them in my 40 acre timber pasture and finish them on my own corn and "walk the corn off the farm." The banker went along since we were in Iowa and that used to be what we did in this part of the world. He loaned me all the money for purchase. Pasture, feed, and feedlot were on me.

A local sale barn owner put together a "lot" of heifers out of Kentucky. Little did I know, the only upright standing two legged humanoid figure these calves had ever seen was either a hungry Bigfoot or an alien doing cattle mutilations. My great plan of rotational grazing using a cross fence of electric wire was wrecked within literal seconds of their escape from the back of the stock trailers. Thank God the line fences held serve! You talk about some sleepless nights, all I could think about was how many counties or states could 5 weight athletic calves cover in one night. I slowly got them to acclimate to me as a helpful human, we kept our buddy Jerome away from the herd as he looked a little too much like Bigfoot. Eventually the herd would come to a feed bunk which I could only occasionally afford to do since I had no money and no corn crop in the bin yet. The calves did well on lush pasture, put good weight on and even impressed Nasty Nelson out of Missouri who had raised quite a few state ribbon winners. We had at least a couple ribbon winners in the bunch, one who won the high jump and kept deciding she needed to be with the neighbors bull "for life" and another who won the prize for bunk walking.

The high jumper who eventually the neighbor kindly purchased from us had a "math problem" when she dropped a perfectly healthy calf when she was supposed to be an open heifer. Turned out it wasn't an attraction to the bull after all, it was her matronly instinct drawing her to the neighbors cow herd, isn't that neat. The bunk walker might have been a genetic mutant hybridized with a goat. She could mount and dismount a feed bunk with perfection, always leaving her trademark excretion right there in the bunk. She caused me enough problem that I had to adapt how I was feeding them, so I overcame that problem by switching to a hillbilly self-feeder, a used hog feeder on a tractor tire, which I could then fill with my combine (yes, the harvesting machine).

25 years later while having a beer at a Christmas party near Bankston Iowa, I found I was credited with inventing the predecessor to the TMR (totally mixed ration) machine which has taken over the industry as the way to feed cattle in a feed bunk system. The old neighborhood calls my John Deere combine the first PMR (partially mixed ration) machine. It worked great for me, I could pull it up next to my grain bin which had an upright unloading auger, while it was slowly filling with corn I could mix in bags of extra protein supplement and minerals, whatever the feed store ration called for. Since it was an old straw walker combine with all that surface area on the back it made a great platform to work from and hike bags to the top of, which I had to do manually since I couldn't afford a loader tractor and had no kids out of diapers yet. It had a manual fold out auger which kept my neck and shoulders proportional to

my gut. The engine sat up front right next to the cab, as it was a John Deere 6600 gasser. The engineers put the engine there so you could see when it was on fire. Had I been thinking even more I could have put a valve on the bottom of the grain tank to run the corn through the combine again to then complete the grind started when I ran it through the field the first time, a function that costs a lot extra on a TMR. Generally speaking the cattle did well for me but did not gain near as fast as ones on a silage ration. I was glad to see TMRs catch on after that, and knew I should have patented the idea.

Thanks to a cooperative neighbor who was a professional at finishing cattle, I got access to a loading chute and a buyer and got mine also sold on the potload type deal. Immediately I put the pencil to it, added up all my costs and figured I made $80 per head on that group of heifers. The banker got paid and seemed happy. I didn't think I got paid enough to justify the risk, so I started asking around about expectations for profit using the "Dick at the end of the lane technique," where first you share a little information and then see what comes back voluntarily. A well established and respected cattle feeder in the area said to me, "$80, you did good, that's the best you'll ever do." That was the official end of my potload cattle feeding days, because $80 times 40 head equals $3200 profit, on an awful lot of risk for a young family. I needed something that would more reliably cash flow. I knew how easily things could have gone the other way, and I don't know if I ever said this....we had no money to lose.

I thought about raising pigs in N.E. Iowa. That thought got snuffed out by "the Dick at the end of the lane." It was the mid-90s, he caught me sneaking down my lane with a bunch of pig feeders I landed at a farm auction, after all, they almost paid me to take those things home. I got scolded for even thinking about it. Thanks to Dick, we avoided the $8 pig disaster. Instead I rented the pasture out to a neighboring dairy farmer family with a bunch of hungry young kids who were just awesome to pick on. That became my lowest risk way to deal with having no money to lose.

13.

Beef, Snarky USDA letter, Country COVID-19

Obviously the margin for feeding beef is very narrow so it becomes a numbers thing, that's why feedlots are mostly talking in the thousands of head instead of hundreds. When the opportunity for reward is kept low enough an individual has no incentive to take risk, then it makes more sense to let someone else own the cattle, then manage the feedlot for a fixed $/head allotment. A big integrator/packer is happy to control that animal all the way through the process, the less free market cattle the better it is for them. The bigger the integrator/packer gets, the more sway they hold in the whole bidding process and eventually they can set the retail price for consumer beef which may have no correlation to the price the independent farmer/rancher receives for the animal, I think that's when you call it monopoly power. We just got done going through all these market inequities and had to ask Universities and Congress for help. We also had to ask: what happened to the Packers and Stockyards (P&S) Act that was supposed to prevent the concentration of power into the hands of so few?

So all of our checkoff dollars and tax money spent at Land Grants have gone toward efficiencies, instead of how to preserve a free, fair and transparent market for independent cattlemen. Checkoff dollars seem to be part of our problem. They come automatically from farmer/rancher to our commodity boards at $1/hd every time a bovine is sold. It behooves the checkoff board to encourage a system in which cattle are sold multiple times because that means more money to work with. Our local sale barn which has many sales of 2000+ head/week and gets to pay this checkoff tax of $2000+ every week. The dollars originate from the farmer/rancher and most of us have become skeptical of just who benefits from this "checkoff", especially after sustaining years of consecutive losses while packers were basking in profits and putting it to the consumers, it's no wonder we started questioning our checkoff investment.

The farmers and ranchers are not the only skeptics here. In 2023 Congress proposed the OFF Act (Senate bill 557), which was supposed to prevent sweetheart deals given to private entities from USDA overseen checkoff programs. The act wanted to prevent checkoffs from being used to contract lobbyists to do work for individual corporations, which you wouldn't think was legal anyway, but that's the kind of stuff D.C. bureaucracies have become accustomed to.

The following email exchange is from questions generated by our new state beef group about specific research being conducted using mRNA type vaccines in our beloved beef. We figure that somehow our own checkoff money is being used to conduct this research, but I can't be sure. Some of the questions were asked from our group's veterinary consultant and translated by me as a proxy. Never anywhere did I represent myself as a Doctor. This is how we are treated by the USDA when we dare to ask, notice the "sir name" used by the USDA employee as he addresses me in the third email.

Hello from rural Iowa,

I am a cow/calf and grain farmer. I am also an officer in a new stockman group called the Iowa Stock Growers Association (ISGA). We understand ISU and or USDA is conducting research into mRNA vaccines in bovines. We would like to know 1.)Is this true? 2.)Are you looking at the human safety aspect of beef from treated animals, and can you provide our group with this peer reviewed research? 3.)Will we know, when we go to a vaccine supplier if the vaccine vial will be identified "mRNA derived source" or marked "traditionally derived source vaccine"? 4.) are you working on withdrawal periods? 5.)How soon will these products hit the market, and will they get full FDA approval or only experimental use permits?

We have to protect the integrity of our USA beef product, and as I'm sure you will agree, need proof of food safety. Thanks.

Dear Dr Savage –

I cannot speak to the situation at ISU, but the CVB has not approved (and does not conduct studies) to vaccinate livestock for COVID-19 and there are no licensed mRNA vaccines for COVID-19 in animals. Additionally, there are no mRNA vaccines being used in cattle in the United States. There are four licensed mRNA vaccines for swine, felines, and canines, but those vaccines have numerous biological differences compared to the COVID-19 mRNA vaccines used in humans. Any vaccine must be thoroughly demonstrated as pure, safe, potent, and effective to receive a license from USDA's Animal and Plant Health Inspection Service (APHIS). Further, there is no requirement or mandate that producers vaccinate their livestock for any disease. It is a personal and business decision left up to the producer and will remain that way.

Thanks

D.V.M., Ph.D.,RBP, DACVM (he/him)
Director - Policy, Evaluation, and Licensing
Center for Veterinary Biologics
National Center for Animal Health

Our beef group interpreted this response as, "just go along boys and girls and '*Dr. Savage*', play nice now. We'll tell you what's good for you." Sounds a little authoritative, even though my question had nothing to do with Covid-19, this respondent with a lot of credentials, got something mixed up in his comprehension and responded strangely going down this Covid-19 diversionary path. Again, I asked nothing about vaccines for Covid-19. Was this an attempt to belittle the question and questioner? Doesn't he know, after being married for 30 years, I'm immune from belittlement. Even though the NCBA, who directs our checkoff dollars admits mRNA vaccine testing has been done for at least a decade now', are we to believe this USDA APHIS director of policy, evaluation, and licensing knows nothing about this research! What do they have to hide. Shouldn't he at least have said, "I can assure you any vaccine derived from mRNA will be identified as such so the farmer/rancher can make an informed choice."

I've had some trouble post vaccination in the past where the thriftiest of calves seem to get an accelerated pneumonia within days of a vaccine, especially when penned up together. If you don't treat them for pneumonia within a half of a day of seeing a dumpy calf, they will up and die on you. I think the experts call this *pathogenic priming*, I call it expensive. Seems like a mutated version of what I was just trying to prevent. The concern for my cattle herd now is that the mutated viruses will shed even more from a mRNA vaccine, requiring booster after booster after booster, just like it did in people. Who wants that?!

A few years ago I changed my system to prevent calves from herding up after vaccination, no problems since. I like my system as it is now and see no need to fix something that is not broken. Maybe the livestock industry should hold off on this new technology until we learn more from the people experiment. Not sure I can afford to use my herd as a test population. In the very least, farmers and ranchers should know what kind of vaccine they are using and traditional vaccines should not be obsoleted.

As I have mentioned before, a statistical factoid that frustrates a lot of us in the cattle industry is that the U.S. imports more beef than it exports. We have been told other countries are already using the mRNA vaccine technology in beef with apparently no scientific testing on changes to human food and safety and because we do not have MCOOL there is no way to know what country your beef comes from. When we ask our own food safety groups to prove it safe, they treat us like Flat Earthers instead of giving us links to the research that proves their assertions. Inquiring minds want to know. Especially inquiring minds who produce food products for a living. Just like we were skeptical about Covid protocols, we are also skeptical when USDA scientists tell us to just go along and play nice. Can you blame us?

Many of us remember the story of DDT. A revolutionary new "first chemical insecticide" brought big time into the U.S. Ag. market after WWII, then used quite extensively up to its cancellation in 1972. Its good side was that it killed mosquitoes carrying malaria and body lice carrying typhus. Its bad side was that it had effects on human reproduction and adverse effects on wildlife. In a lesson at the big football U we reviewed Rachael Carson's book *Silent Spring* and they used it to teach us how some pesticides can bioaccumulate in animal and fish fats and get passed up the food chain and really get concentrated in "top of the food chain" predatory birds, which is apparently exactly what happened to eagles. Fish must have been an efficient mechanism for bioaccumulation and since eagles

D. C. Savage

eat fish, then the eggs shells would weaken in the nest and the birds would crush their own eggs as a result of this particular chemical. Not good for the propagation of the species, hence the book title *Silent Spring*. Now we know why eagles have made such an amazing comeback. No doubt this chemical was very useful for humans settling in the swampy parts of the country, but it took us a while to figure out what its bad faults were. Maybe this event in the modern science era gives us farmers a healthy dose of skepticism when it comes to adopting the first go around of a new type of technology.

Yes, most farmers and ranchers do use vaccines for herd management of clostridial and respiratory diseases, so you wouldn't exactly call us antivax. Additionally, some of us choose to vaccinate for other conditions like pinkeye and calf scours (diarrhea), some of us do not, leaving these lower risk conditions to natural resistance, or "treat the sick" as a herd health philosophy. It looks like our livestock health care industry wants to take us away from a "treat the sick" philosophy to a "vaccinate every animal for every risk philosophy". To be skeptical here, getting a needle in every animal might be more profitable for them than getting to treat perhaps one out of 25. According to a quick web search (Globenewswire), the animal vaccine market is expected to double by 2030. Follow the money. Could the move by the USDA to get RFID (Radio-Frequency IDentification) tags in all our animals work hand and glove with this new livestock health philosophy, where access to a market requires vaccines logged on an RFID tag, subject to site assessment audits by a third party. What other onerous ways could RFID tags be used? Genomic information logged onto these tags may be used to box us into having to use "their" genetic lines resulting in consolidation of genetics like the pork industry has done.

Could these RFID tags also be used to log carbon scores so that cattle having too much gas coming out of either end, or having the wrong environmental indices logged from inputs, get themselves on a path to termination. In an article posted June 2, '23, in VisionTimes.com, 200,000 Irish cattle will have to be culled or euthanized in the next three years to meet climate

102

goals, and it looks like Ireland's mandatory RFID tags are part of this plan. I think abuse of this technology is highly likely and our new Iowa beef group opposes the "mandated" use of these electronic identification tags.

The above scenarios are entirely possible and if this is the future of beef, I may transition back toward more row crop. Maybe that is exactly the reaction the USDA wants, more people get out. At least we have assurance from the officially sanctioned Vet. Dr. at the USDA that vaccines in livestock are voluntary and intend to remain so. I am glad this is their official position, in writing. Now let's make sure the consumers (farmers and ranchers)of livestock vaccines know what they are getting.

So how bad are cow farts? I can assure you, they do happen and you better not trust them after that first day you turn the cows out on lush green cover crops. I recommend a 10 foot setback zone while working with these "green" cattle at least from the back end of the cow. Oh, and watch the wind too! Cows also belch and amaze me how their rumen just keeps on doing its thing, chewing their cud, using a four compartment stomach and all those other organs to take low cost feeds all the way to a superior human protein source, something that cannot be replicated in a lab vat for an imitation meat type food. Methane gas is blamed for having 28 times more global warming potential than CO_2, so cows are a favorite target for greenies who have not taken the time to review the science as presented by U.C. Davis, CLEAR Center, July 2020. They report that the kind of biogenic methane from cows cycles rapidly, calling it an SLCP (short lived climate pollutant) less persistent and damaging than fossil fuel methane emissions, therefore declaring global warming from cow methane as "neutral".

If I'm interpreting all of this correctly, my cows are consuming CO_2 that got turned into cellulose stored away in plants during photosynthesis, they belch some methane out of the rumen and within 12 years this atmospheric methane is converted back to CO_2 through "hydroxyl oxidation" and trapped again by plants for a beautiful non-global warming biogenic carbon cycle. If this biogenic carbon cycle concept is all true, greenhouse gas(GHG) emissions from cows are grossly overstated, which would make sense, because that's how the greenies scare people into thinking everything used to sustain the current human population is evil.

If you would like to avoid duking the gaseous cow thing out in the arena of science, then let's try reason. According to Google's little blurb written April 12, '23, taken from USDA-ARS: "Life cycle annual GHG emissions related to beef production and consumption in the U.S. is about 250 Tg or 3.7% of the total national GHG emission inventory." Now, if we were to accept the 3.7% number for beef, who wouldn't be o.k. with that kind of trade-off for a wonderful and significant food protein source. You can't run extruders and vats and build manufacturing plants to make fake meat for no carbon expenditure either. You especially aren't going to do the fake meat thing on a middle class farm with a few gates, a pickup truck w/stock trailer, barb wire, hedge posts and a new edition thesaurus (so we can come up with new cuss words when working or chasing cattle).

Curiosity has me looking at the size of the bison herd, pre-industrial evil man. According to a web search, Statista says we currently have 28 million beef cows, USDA says 28.2. A different site, Ozark bison, claims there were 60 million bison in year 1800, 40 million in 1830, 35.6 million in 1840, and 5 million in 1870. Bison are also ruminants and at one time may have tripled the size of our current beef cow herd. Good thing the Indians didn't put RFID tags in them or else John Kerry and the Green New Dealers would have had the information necessary to euthanize them for "prairie gas" emissions. I guess the green new dealers are too young for that, only John Kerry was around for the buffalo.

14.

Some Wins in the Beef Arena and the Winner T-bone

Please keep in mind, the reason I address beef so much is because it is the last of the major meats to offer the independent farmers and ranchers a mortgage lifter type livestock entity, a very important component of many small and mid-sized farms. Niche markets do exist in any of the meats but beef is still in the fight for mainstream independent markets.

Multinational packers increase imports whenever the price of our cattle get too high, using foreign cattle as a buffer against high prices, also using any supply "hitch" like the Holcomb packing plant fire or Covid to crank the price up on the consumer and run the price down on the independent producers of cattle. As I have said earlier, 85% of cattle are processed by the big four packers and they have a powerful lobbying group. Since MCOOL was shot down in 2015 the farmer/rancher percent of the consumer beef retail value fell to 37% in 2020, amidst record packer profits, leaving us cow pokes all spinning to find a fix, we even got the attention of some legislators until the next crisis came along, and then the next, and then the next......

Maybe we did get somewhere with all the attention focused on cattle markets because on 6/22/22 the Senate gave us the *Bi-*

partisan meat packers' special investigators act. Thanks to Senators; Chuck Grassley (IA), Jon Tester (MO) and Mike Round (SD). Ever since then, things have been a little better for the cow/calf guys and I think for the independent feedlots also, I know the packers are not hogging as much of the profit pie now. Can we keep profit for all of us is the question.

Two other wins for the independent cattlemen have come recently, according to R-CALF USA, on Nov.9th, '23 the USDA AMS (Ag Marketing Service) announced that it is, "clarifying that the domestic origin requirements for meat purchased by the agency for nutrition assistance programs must be from animals that are born, raised and slaughtered in the United States." THANKS! Maybe we can replace some of those "fudge rounds" with "Product of USA" meats hopefully without the ultra-processing. All of us independents have been asking for this and applaud the USDA and some of our Beef groups for getting it done.

Another win for the mortgage lifter cattle herd comes from Sen. Tester (D-MT) and Sen. Round (R-SD) at the end of Jan. '24, called "the School Lunch Integrity Act of 2024". The act would federally ban the use of cell-based meat substitutes in school lunches, following attempts by Florida and Arizona to ban them on a state-by-state basis. The rationale being, food safety studies of allergens and nutrition have not been adequately re-searched, and that our kids' lunch rooms should not be used as a test lab. They forgot to mention the fact that they probably also taste like sh..! Where were they back in the old soy-burger days when the lunch room would erupt in a teen taste rebellion, pounding the lunch tables to the beat of "We Will, We Will, ROCK YOU!" Usually started by the stoners, then the nerds joined, then the college preppers, even the FFA'ers got involved in this "bonding of belligerence" moment. Sure did make me appreciate my packed lunch.

Even though we do not have MCOOL back yet, we are getting a little help now from Congress. In the recent past we had some support from our Congressmen to promote the 50/14 concept where 50% of cattle would have to be purchased from the "cash trade" market and then that trade would have to be negotiated within 14 days. Ironically our support gets derailed by some of the big beef groups who have memberships and support coming from the packer side of the argument, unfortunately those big groups are in control of where our checkoff money goes to research and advertise beef. Also, the 50/14 "independent cattlemen" movement got derailed by Farm Bureau who has a national scope and when addressing this issue at a national meeting, their southern constituency likes the status quo and they will not support the free market cash trade 50/14 idea. Who needs friends like these.

Quite a few farmers and ranchers are so discouraged and credit to them, they have big plans to process their own beef. I've been there, done that, and it did make me appreciate the capacity our packing industry and marketers can achieve, they all add value in their own capacity. I personally prefer to see them do their job, I do mine, and all of us play the game fair. I'm afraid the only way to do that is through P&S act regulations and at least the new special investigator to the attorney general may help accomplish that. In the meantime, please buy from the independent farmers and ranchers where you can at least identify what country your beef is from, and determine what production system or genetics you want.

Some interesting beef eating factoids. First on the ever popular T-bone steak. They taste great! The small side of the T is the filet mignon from that inner loin muscle, it is super tender. The big side of the T has more flavor but slightly less tender, in this part of the country when it is cut away from the bone, they call it a K.C. strip steak. Go to your local butcher and see if you can get some "Product of the USA Beef" and prove me right. The excellent rib-eye steak is right between the two on tenderness and tastiness, I like the bone-in type better, you can even get these with a tomahawk looking rib bone, satisfying that primal man instinct with a primal meat cut. The sirloin steak is a big, almost as good steak that is versatile and often feeds our kids who need more protein volume but slightly less tender, a big hit for the kids getting their WFFP meal. Ask the butcher about a relative newcomer to the industry, the flat iron steak, you'll just start grinning when you get hit with that flavor bomb and tender too, add that one to your list. The chuck is my favorite roast, but that new Instant Pot we got for Christmas can take any of the lower quality cheaper roasts and make them fall apart and tender, and get it done fast. I wish my Mom could have used one of these Instant Pot machines, as the crock pot was her go-to for roasts.

Speaking of cheap protein, vitamins and minerals. Hamburger, I figured out a different way to make it, called "Rolled Roast Burger Steaks," we just call them RRBs. Take your frozen one pound tube of ground beef straight out of the freezer and just simply grill it. Take the plastic wrapper off first of course, then put it straight on the grill (the beef, not the plastic kids), it actually stays together, cooks all the way through and develops a "bark" on the outside. I use what we figure is 85% lean hamburger from our own beef. It will take at least 2 beverages to get it done, but watch for juices to start running and let them roll out for a bit, I like mine rare to medium rare. The cheaper your supplier, the longer I would cook it. Have one roll to experiment with for doneness and the other roll for sliders. Bet you'll never get that first roll to a bun. Season with anything you like. You can thank me later, grill master.

On the radio recently was a story about a Vegan restaurant adding meat back to the menu. I get that, because as much as I like plants (accept Giant Ragweed/waterhemp/cocklebur/velvetleaf…), when I have a physically taxing day, nothing will keep me going as long as meat protein. I also think it is brain food. Seems like the body will start craving beef, you have a good meal of it, then the next day it seems your hunger stays at bay. Looking up why this is, it appears to come down to mainly two nutrients readily available in beef. It's a very good source of iron which helps blood carry oxygen. Also, B12 content is very high, helping with the brain fog and energy levels. These are only two of the 10 essential nutrients bodily available in beef. Available in a way superior to vitamins in the pill form.

I realize some people are not able to eat mammalian meat because of AGS (Alpha-Gal Syndrome) which is normally associated with a bite from the lone star tick as a carrier. I feel sorry for those afflicted with AGS. Unfortunately this syndrome will result in an allergic reaction to some meats. Blood tests can confirm the diagnosis looking for specific antibodies. Those darn tics! Maybe wild turkeys do serve a purpose, go ahead, cluck and clack and eat those tics, just stay out of my corn!

As a farmer, something else I think is really neat about the two meat animals I've raised the most, both Cow/calf and Boer goats (we had up to 200 of these meat type goats when the kids were young), both types can utilize low quality forage and less productive acres while converting it to awesome people food, almost always helping the land reduce the advance of the wasteful, sticker bushes! Every farm I've had, has non-tillable areas that you wouldn't exactly consider timber, places where the cow is better than the plow. You can't fence hogs on it, they will root it up. Chickens would fly over the fence or get eaten by the fox. Sheep won't eat the sticker bushes, but coyotes will eat the sheep (you know the story by now, "eat lamb, 10s of thousands of coyotes can't be wrong"). Cows or goats with a protector dog, are the perfect fit. Although I prefer eating beef, goat meat isn't bahhhhhhhhhhhd!

15.

Rookie Lobbyist Goes to D.C.

Speaking of sticker bushes, I put myself through the agony of a trip to D.C. to sell the HFSA concept outlined below. You can brief through the outline I gave to them as I have already laid out some of the HFSA concepts earlier. Please take a minute to read the example. I wasn't sure how to go about pitching this new concept, so I decided to give them something they've never seen before, only one page! (Obamacare 9625 pages of rules, approx. 20,000 pages of associated regulations). That's not fair of me. This one pager was only a proposal and an outline, not a whole bill. My point is…. that a significant shift in farm policy philosophy could be done very simply through alterations of existing tax policy. We wouldn't even need a complicated farm bill. Can anything in that town be simple?

Hybrid Farm Savings Account (HFSA)

Proposal: Congress should modify current tax code to give farmers a tax preferred account that looks much like the Health Savings Account. This HFSA would allow a farmer to put $20,000 (before tax) or up to ½ of allowable 179 tax deduction into a designated HFSA account in a local bank. The account can be accessed anytime, but only tax free when the county is declared a disaster area, otherwise rules of a traditional IRA apply as we age and use residual for retirement. It would be advised for crop farmers to couple this with catastrophic crop insurance. Livestock/hay/vegetable/etc.farmers who have been left out of big programs would now have a way to buffer tough times. Long term, this model may be able to replace other USDA programs and ultimately save taxpayers money and reduce the federal deficit. What makes this version of a savings account so much more powerful than previous versions is the access to ½ of allowable 179. Banks should be required to pay prime minus 2 for these accounts. Just like the HSA, approved soil "wellness" activities should be able to come from these accounts tax free.

Example: Farmer Joe has a good financial year in 2016 and has $100,000 he could take a 179 deduction on. Instead of using all of this on farm machinery again, he funds his HFSA account at the local bank for $50,000 and spends $50,000 on equipment.

In 2017 Joe has a break-even year but his great uncle left him $30,000 so he was able to put $20,000 of this into his HFSA account tax free. He now has $70,000 plus a little interest in this account.

In 2018 Joe has a drought and has a $60,000 loss after his catastrophic crop insurance pays out. The county was declared a disaster area so he could pull out of his HFSA to cover the loss without paying tax.

In 2028 Joe retires with 250,000 in his HFSA, he now pays tax on his withdrawals as if it was a traditional IRA.

Note to Policy Makers: Think of the huge transition of farms and farmland coming. This account would help a young person working that off farm job transition from a hobby farm to full-time, we all know his/her biggest obstacle is capital. Help us help ourselves.

My efforts to impact change in Farm policy may have been time wasted to date, I guess that is why I write this book. Frustrated that Farm policy really has nothing to do with what farmers want. Farm policy gets formulated by what lobbyists want and by what the government wants, it's completely top down. An example of this comes from my interaction with the Farm Bureau organization. Locally we have some of the nicest people representing the Bureau's many assorted business interests. They sell us all kinds of insurances, Home insurance, Car insurance, Life insurance, Health insurance, Farm liability insurance, Nursing home insurance, and Crop insurance to name a few. They even do financial investing services and some financial education, etc. I'm not trying to be an expert in their businesses, but I do know they would be hard to compete against because they are a real force in rural America. An important part of their business model is collecting membership dues to the Farm Bureau which in '23 cost us $45 (Ohio $90, if you give to the Political Action Committee, which they autobill for). Dues then give you the right to do business with them. Go ahead, ask yourself, "why would anyone pay for the 'opportunity' to do business with a company"? Well you'll pay if they are the only game in town, and you'll pay for the convenience of multiple services especially when coupled with good local people. The dues are memberships, and membership numbers are key to Farm Bureau's power as a lobbyist in Washington D.C. It's a brilliant business model, and you can't blame them when they leverage that huge membership and hire lobbyists to represent legislation which enhances their business interest. Example: Crop Insurance, any company selling it benefits from an increasing commitment from the government to subsidize it.

Earlier in this book I mentioned an interaction maybe 8 years ago when a Sen. Grassley aide told me they liked the idea of my proposed Hybrid Farm Savings Account (HFSA) but couldn't do anything without it first being written up by the Farm Bureau and evaluated by a Land Grant. When I stop to think about that position, it sickens me. I know that is what our government has become, but there is nothing right about it. We must all remind them, "the Farm Bureau is not your constituency and does not represent me or rural America regardless of the size of its membership, they are a big business with awesome lobbying power and they have legitimate reasons to represent themselves for profit motives". Many of us are amazed and disgusted at the power Farm Bureau has with Congress. If only I had that kind of power, it would be daylight savings time all year round.

I sort-of listened to the legislative aide and researched what it would take to influence the Farm Bureau through their grass roots system. I took three years to promote the idea of an HFSA at local county Farm Bureau meetings only to watch it go to the state convention and get some votes here and there, but no support from the top. I wrote to their "grassroots" website, where they request input from the people....again, nothing. It seemed strange that when I would run the idea independently past fellow farmers they would ask me how to get this kind of account, or in one case the farmer said, "it's such a no-brainer, I'm ashamed I didn't think of this first." Our beef Cow/Calf group advanced this HFSA concept along in our list of "asks" to our Congressmen, especially interested because Cow/Calf farmers and ranchers have been left out of most mainstream government programs and this HFSA would give them their own "liquid" rainy day fund.

I've determined an idea is like a grass's root, it needs water and nutrients. After a few years and some final phone calls I realized the Farm Bureau will never water or feed my grass's roots. On my last ditch phone call to Farm Bureau D.C. this authoritative lady helped me decide, OK I'm done now! The conversation was kind of like hitting your head against a brick wall, only it was those kind of bricks that have straight vertical texture grooves on them. She kept telling me over and over again that Farm Bureau already has policy supporting farm savings accounts, but when I desperately attempted to explain that the HFSA was a tax advantaged concept which made it totally different from a normal savings account, she said again, "we already have Policy supporting farm savings accounts." I truly believe she was not an A.I. robot, but I can't count out a human/Reptilian hybrid with ice water coursing through her veins, and a very large paycheck.

I spent $300 of my own money to book a round trip flight to D.C. By this time, I have given up on the grassroots process, so instead, let's try explaining this in person to legislators. Luckily my D.C. trip coincided with an exiting flight for my Mother-in-Law, whose endearing nickname is WWE, which stands for Wicked Witch of the East. She would be disappointed in me for not mentioning her in this fun light. We were both flying out of Des Moines where she helped me get on this democratic (as in democracy) airline that used some weird system for seating which eventually made sense to me thanks to WWE. We were not departing on the same plane as she would be returning to Cleveland by broom (all you guys can borrow that one!)

The whole flying experience is nerve racking because there are people at an airport. Nerve racking because I was going to have to get a cab, which I've never done ever…. that I can remember. Nerve racking because the Top Gun pilot thought he'd push a passenger airline right up against mechanical limitations as he banked it hard to land at Ronald Reagan Airport, I saw a lot of wing flex since the wing was about all I could see until we got totally vertical and D.C. looked really big for a minute. Reminded me of one of those swingy roller coaster rides, just wasn't expecting all that fun out of a plane ride. He told me afterward, they have to do that hard right to avoid restricted air space over D.C., I told him exactly what row and aisle they would need to clean up. If only tractors could fly!

Safely on the ground in D.C. My first cab ride ever, and the guy is wearing very non-traditional American attire, especially on his head, probably not the best choice for professional work wear when you're hauling visitors around D.C. post 9/11. There was a thick language barrier, but he eventually figured out my dialect. I was successful in communicating a desired drop off point. He in turn delivered me swiftly and competently to the back of the Senate office building for such a reasonable fee I don't even remember. What I do remember from that ride was how modern and clean and not busy everything looked, at least from the perspective of the highway, it didn't look like a lot of the industrial cities I'm used to, where the drive to a river grain terminal takes you through a tough part of town. D.C. looked a little soft. I imagine they did not "defund the police" in D.C. Another thing they did not defund was the crane companies. There were building projects everywhere, but the buildings were shorter than the tall buildings you see in Chicago or Cleveland, guess that's why you can see all the cranes. No wonder all those USDA employees didn't want to move their offices to Kansas City, not enough cranes in the whole midwest.

The office building I entered was not short on security and I did happen to notice they had pistols, which I assume contained live rounds with unexpired gunpowder. After all the body scanning x-rays checked out, I entered the hallway and from that point on became officially disoriented for the rest of the day. Walking down the hallway wondering why the heck I was doing all this, I had to remind myself that we the people run and own all of government. As trite as that sounds, it is the truth; of the people, by the people, and for the people. They serve us, we do not serve them. Let's just hope this is not a *Soylent Green* (Charlton Heston's not best dystopian movie, 1973) type of serving event.

The hallways echoed emptiness. I reckoned there was a lot going on behind all those 12' tall doors "fit for giants," it was an institutional feeling work environment. I met up with a group of renewable energy tax credit lobbyists who were using me to gain access to our state representatives and I was using them to find my way around. Both of our pitches had to do with tax law and agriculture, so we complemented one another. I was never promised a face to face with either Senator but in both cases I was told "it's possible." So as you might imagine, we got their Farm Aids. It's very possible the Senators never even got a schedule with our proposed meeting on it. At their offices I noticed the D.C. staffers are a little distant from really knowing and understanding their constituency, the farm staffers being the exception.

Our meetings felt productive, no, let's say attentive. We shared time between the two groups laying out our desires, the renewables group had a professional and I had me. The pro lady representing the renewable group was organized/efficient/put together and probably did not come cheap. It wouldn't surprise me if at one time she hasn't lobbied each side of any one issue. I got the biggest kick out of how she would switch shoes before entering a Senator's office, so there was one pair of shoes to walk the halls and another to go into offices....now that's professional! The boots I wore were much more versatile, they could go in the barn, the feed store, the bank, Congress, and then back to the barn again to clean the Congress off of them.

Something I cannot figure out after the fact is the whole campaign contribution money thing. I was asked by a friend slightly experienced in lobbying with an industry trade group,"did you give them a campaign finance contribution?"

My response to him was something like this; "Heck no, there wasn't even enough money left in my budget to get an $11 cheese burger or $3 water at the airport." The airports could do a lot better at providing water fountains. They herd you around like cattle, they should at least water you like one. Anyway, I never did see any money or opportunity for money to be exchanged, but would I even know how all of that is done. Seriously, I hope that the government we get is not dictated by the funding they get, I try not to be that cynical….so I looked it up on the net.

Hold onto your hats folks, because your hair is about to stand on end! I found an overwhelming amount of influencers have contributed to some of these Senator re-election campaign funds. One Senator, who I consider squeaky clean, has 92 pages of contributors at 100 contributors per page. Yes, that equals 9200 contributors. All public records. Page one starts with the first normal looking contributor in slot 3 at $76,000 and goes down to the company in slot 100 giving "only" $16,000. 10 pages later, business entities are still contributing $3000 a crack. Jumping all the way to page 40 there are 100 entrants in our money hungry game giving $1000 a pop. Page 80 has the $200 participants and it takes clear to page 90 to start the $35 tightwads. This game would make a mob boss jealous. I'm not accusing the Senator of personally profiting financially from all this campaign money, but it would be impossible to expect any human to not be influenced by such contributions. You could be the patron saint of virtue and still have guilt after a day in this town. Who authorized such a stupid system? The system is so bad I wonder if our country can make it past its 250 year semiquincentennial coming in 2026.

I don't pretend to know anything about how the game is played, what I do know is that the other half of my lobbying duo was successful and I was not….that "L" trend continues! Not even a scintilla of love for my pet idea has been shown from anyone with the power to do anything, not even from the conservative think tank groups, by the way, what exactly is it that the Heritage foundation does? Yet every year we get to tax time and wish we could use the "179" to put some "liquidity" type money away for ourselves instead of enriching the equipment manufacturers. But I saw a lot of these equipment manufacturers early in that 92 page list of donors, Hmmm!

I got done with the meetings at both Senator's offices and got the same elated feeling of being done with school on a sunny spring Friday afternoon....yes, I'm outta here! The new cab driver was destined to be my long lost buddy. There were 50 cabs to choose from, how do you pick? One Prius after another, so I picked a Prius. The driver had a great attitude and asked me, "vvwhere are you going," I told him "airport" and he asked which one. Dummy me, not realizing I was in a multiple airport town, I had to look at my ticket to know which one, proving that day I was an "Idiot Out Wandering Around (I.O.W.A.)" He couldn't believe I had just come to town only to leave the same day and not tour around. I couldn't believe I had come to town at all.

The airport experience may be worth commenting on. For sure I did not want to interact with people earlier that morning on my way out, plus I had an excuse because WWE was helping me get around. But, on the return trip with a heavy load lifted, I wouldn't have minded a little conversation with a stranger, especially to get a gauge on political opinion or just what kind of business they were conducting in D.C. I know most of them would have said, "if I tell you, I'll have to shoot you." I was prepared to use the line, "what were you doing in the swamp today – you do not look like an alligator." I'm here to tell you, casual conversation is not what it used to be, where's John Candy when you need him? The smartphone is a phenomenon! Anyone and almost everyone is holding that device right in front of them at all times using it as a shield against the outside world. What an incredible tool for withdrawal. I became self-conscious that my flip phone was inadequate. What if it rings and I pull it out of my pocket. Would the act of going to your pocket cause a youngster to call airport security, or maybe a stock ringtone or flip open get you surrounded by hecklers. If you want to see something incredible, watch people, all with heads down walk through an airport without even walking into one another. Talent everywhere! I'm convinced the best new phones have an app called the "Bat app," where they use bat type sonar to avoid collision, it must vibrate left softly for "glide left," or vibrate left violently to steer you "hard left"; like our Federal Government.

I can usually strike up a conversation with a fence post, however, I managed to speak to no one all the way home. No one seemed accessible and by the time we were getting on the plane at St. Louis heading home to Des Moines, I'm not sure I was accessible either. Would I do it again....not unless I could recalibrate for low expectations, so I guess I'm saying, there's a chance. As for now I'd rather give the $300 to my kids to pay down on the $250,000 federal debt currently on their heads. I hear this question all the time out here in flyover country, "How we gonna make it?"

16.

Where Does the HFSA Idea
Go from Here?

Now we get to my main motive for writing this book, I write hoping to find help with the HFSA concept. I really don't know where help even comes from, so as a last chance promotion attempt I will channel my inner farmer and "seed the idea", and see if it grows. Somehow we need to start getting away from big spending and intrusive government policies. Why not start with the independent minded people who make up agriculture, use farmers and ranchers as a test population, most of them I know would love to see less "help" from government. Quoting Ronaldus Maximus, "the nine most terrifying words in the English language are: I'm from the government, and I'm here to help." Most of rural USA agrees.

I've hustled this idea about as much as I have time and resources to do. My focus has to be on family and farm business, so all other things have to be relegated to hobby status. I'm appealing here for help, although I do not know what help looks like; just hoping it doesn't look like a straightjacket.

From my promotional activities to date I have come to realize that part of the problem with grasping the HFSA concept has been the lack of general understanding of how a

Health Savings Account (HSA) works, and since it is part of the Hybrid Concept, it helps if I explain it. I had an "aha" moment when pitching the HFSA idea to a prominent private University professor in rural America. I could tell he had only a vague understanding of how HSA's work. I found it strange that such a commonly used health care system in rural America would not be well understood by college educators, yet for us practitioners to survive the insanely high costs of health insurance we were forced to understand it and in many cases adopt these HSA's. I get it, had you been offered full coverage health insurance your whole career, this HSA concept may not resonate because you never needed to consider it as an option.

Generally speaking, the HSA is an account set up by your local bank which will accept money earmarked for health care expenditures so that you can reduce your income, hence saving on taxes. This account is committed to healthcare and sanctioned by the IRS via tax law and was one of the best things to come out of the George Bush junior administration. In 2023 you are allowed up to $7300 per family of "before tax income" to be put away in this special account. This account can then be coupled with a "catastrophic insurance policy", meaning one with a high deductible and hopefully a low out-of-pocket cap. The beauty of high deductible health care plans is that the insured then has a vested interest in his/her health, the difficulty comes from chronic health problems where you spend your deductible every year.

Prior to Obamacare this type of insurance fit our farm's needs perfectly with a reasonable $300ish/month premium, then after Obamacare it started to skyrocket to $900+/month for catastrophic insurance which is when we were finally priced out of the private health care rolls unfortunately and into the "Exchange" Obamacare set up. We still use the HSA account to do almost all of our farm's healthcare "actual costs" but now the "Exchange" determines a subsidy based on our income and we select a huge deductible like $5700 per person/$11,400 per year max catastrophic policy in case the farm makes a lot of money. If the farm business has a good income year we could get back taxed or penalized to the tune of $1400/month for the policy we chose, that's $16,800/year to get a high deductible crappy health plan!

It used to be simpler and more predictible before the Obamacare subsidy game started. There used to be more health care providers in the state and more competition for rates. Health Care is a good example of how big government programs start with subsidies and design winners who become too big to fail, all the while increasing costs and slipping toward the ultimate goal of a government run system, in health care the ultimate goal is a "single payer system" which means socialized medicine. Another example of slipping away from capitalism toward socialism....sounds like farming, sounds like banking, unless we can stop it.

I liked the pre-Obamacare system better and wish all states would have been required to have a pool for the pre-existing condition problem. When we moved, Ohio had an entirely reasonable system in place. Jill had a pre-existing condition called pregnancy (yes, I checked the line fence). We had to commit to x number of months of supplemental state sponsored high risk insurance, or get a midwife. We chose the ~$800/month route and insured against problems in the pregnancy which thankfully did not occur until the kid left home at age 18 and left us down another good farm hand. I feel bad for those who have fallen through the cracks in any of the systems, since it seems a system cannot be designed without flaws. One of the flaws of the past seems that numerous times I was told about people getting kicked out of their insurance pools for a bout of illness. Isn't that why we have insurance and why actuaries have a job. An insurance company shouldn't be able to manipulate clientele after the fact to exclude risk. For this reason government regulators do have a role to play in insurance, also in banking to keep investment and speculative banking separate from consumer banking, and on highways to have a speed limit, and at grain elevators to keep them from speculating with grain owned by farmers, and in beef to keep monopolies from abusing ranchers and consumers....etc.

Full health care coverage seems like a thing of the past unless you work for the government or a fortune 500. Everyone should have skin in the game, so a tax deferred Health Savings Account coupled w/high deductible insurance is a good option, especially for us independents. A person does not want to overfund the HSA account because there will be little reward as an interest bearing account, since it only gives you checkbook rates, which are next to nothing. At Age 65 you can no longer fund the HSA, you can keep withdrawing for qualified medical expenses within limits. Also at age 65 you can start withdrawing for any use penalty free, but not tax free. Please do not use this text for tax advice.

I brief though all of this because it helps to understand the Hybrid Farm Savings Account (HFSA) as I have proposed it. Putting *skin-in-the-game* money in a bank account designed for farm expenditures to be taken out tax free for intended uses like "Governor declared emergencies" or even soil health expenditures like "Cover cropping" or "filter strips". One might parallel some of these practices to getting well care check-ups covered in health care.

One morning during chores, when I have some of my clearest thoughts, I had an epiphany, a brilliant thought, a revelation, whatever you want to call it, **why not steal the HSA concept and adapt it for the farm.**

Coupled with catastrophic crop insurance you can see where the farmer could use this kind of HFSA account to cover the "deductible" in a year where drought or monsoon damages his crop or livestock. I'm arguing for that money to have *liquidity* and be capable of coming out of the HFSA account tax free if it is used for "emergency or other approved use". The amount withdrawn tax free should be limited to annual losses. Coupled with catastrophic crop insurance it provides a rainy day fund for a business that can really suffer from excessive rain or the opposing drought.

Let's say Farmer A has a 50% crop insurance plan, his established field yield (APH) is 180 bushel/A, so he is guaranteeing himself 90 bu/A of production. Say drought hits and the field yields 70 bu/a, so Farmer A has a 20 bushel loss multiplied by a theoretical fall price of $5.00/bushel equaling $100/A coming from crop insurance (we call this an indemnity payment). Let's approximate he still has a deficit of $300/acre, leaving him short of meeting financial obligations on 1000 acres of corn, that's $300,000 he needs to just pay the bills. Hopefully he has seriously funded that HFSA account or maybe Uncle Richy Rockefeller will answer his phone call and give out some jingle. Now, let's go to 10,000 acres and the deficit goes to $3,000,000. Not chump change, now you're going to start thinking about how many acres you really want, how much risk, how many calls to Uncle Richy. Under our current subsidized crop insurance system, Uncle Richy is not necessary because, Uncle Sam covers almost all $3 million in losses. Yes mob bosses, this racket can be run within a legal framework. Now you know why farming big is exploding.

Our current system of high subsidies to crop insurance and high revenue guarantees (up to 90%) have taken a lot of the risk out of farming big in row crop corn, soybeans and wheat. Not a soul can deny that, and this factoid alone should reveal how Crop Insurance has distorted the economic balance on the farm. This year(2023) crop insurance has paid many farmers who have had a pretty good year, the highest I've heard is a farmer getting paid for a loss when his yield was 208 bu/A., (~4%) above the state average. That's from a Revenue Assurance type Multi Peril policy. Bet the equipment manufacturers like that!

The question is, at what level of coverage does crop insurance begin to tamper with a free and open marketplace? I suppose a purist would say, "any crop insurance interferes with economic balance." I'm not quite a purist, so I would argue that the Health Savings Account (HSA) had the correct theory in designing an account that would complement catastrophic health insurance. So, "catastrophic" for row crops in my opinion would include plans for crop insurance which insure up to 60%, and no more. Rates should be determined just like rates for hail insurance, where rate reflects risk based on field history, regional history, and amount of insurance coverage desired. Crop insurance rates in plains states which have more risk should be higher than rates in the "I" states (see following map). No more insuring a Corvette for the price of a Chevette. They may both be "Vette's", but they are not equals. Trust me, I know, in no way would a

Corvette make as good a pickup truck as a Chevette!

Looking at that last thought a little closer. The guy driving the Corvette may be more likely to lay a burnout in the school parking lot making him a higher risk than the Chevette guy, especially since the Chevette couldn't even do a burnout with greased tires. A guy driving a Corvette has his car repaired after an accident, making him more expensive, because he doesn't want a broken chunk of fiberglass hurting his chances to find love eternal, whereas the guy in the Chevette gave up on love eternal years ago. You get where I've digressed to. The insurance companies know our personalities and associated risks before we do, and bake it into rates. Why shouldn't that be the case for Crop Insurance? I guarantee it would if the government were not subsidizing it.

I said earlier in the book that an insurance company CEO assured me they were doing something in crop insurance to make rates reflect risk. Maybe they did, but it still fell way short. To illustrate that point I get the following information from an awesome analysis done via a collaborative effort between University of Illinois and Ohio State, published in U of I's Farm Doc Daily June 27, '23. Called, "Premium Support and Crop Insurance: An analysis of the proposed 4% Farm Premium Cap." So let's look for farmer premiums similar to the $14/A I pay for unsubsidized 55% insurance. Information gleaned from their charts show that a farmer from central Illinois "best dirt ever" Mclean Co. pays $12/Acre with a $25/A "premium subsidy (P.S.)" from the taxpayers, giving the farmer 80% enterprise unit type insurance coverage. In Richland Co. North Dakota you would have to bump down slightly to 75% coverage to stay around $14/A, with a $47 P.S. from the taxpayer. And in irrigated Sherman Co. Texas 75% coverage would cost you $15/A (with a $50 P.S.). All these products look about the same cost to the farmer with similar coverage, resulting in an economic incentive to get more acres into row crop production in the higher risk areas. This is a total distortion of normal economic principles, just look at the premium subsidies (P.S.) taxpayers are required to give! And get this; in the conclusion, paper authors say it may not be a good idea to lower these farmer premiums to a 4% cap because it might be too advantageous to the marginal production areas, and I can definitely agree. But how can they ignore the obvious flaw in the existing design....rates do not reflect risk. That's why we end up with indemnity (payment to farmer) maps that too often look like these below. Take one more leap in the logic flow and you also realize that it's not only the taxpayer subsidizing farming on marginal acres, it's the Mclean Co. Illinois farmer who is subsidizing his own competition in the plains states. I'm not saying the Plains states should not produce corn, just that rates to the farmer should reflect risk. Then the ranchers will have a shot at competing for land and the cowman and the farmer can be friends once again.

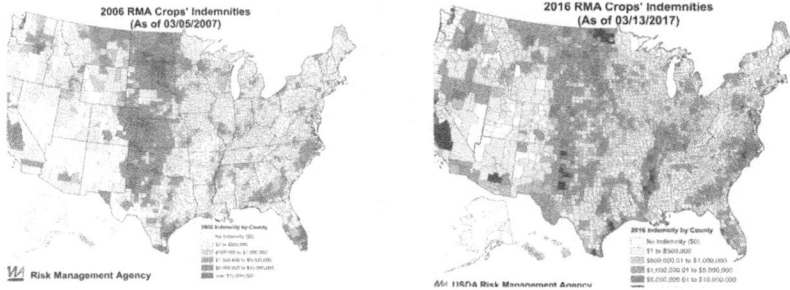

'06 an '16 maps Crop insurance indemnity maps.

Hail insurance has always operated independent of subsidies, so we know crop insurance can. The insurance companies are not dumb, but they play on the field the government has designed, even if the sod is slippery (a super bowl 2023 reference).

In my own neighborhood, here's how crop insurance increases rental rates for cropland. Keep in mind 68% of Iowa farmland is owned by "other than farmer". For a brief and fleeting moment in my farm life I got on the call list of a farm manager. This guy did a really good job of getting the land-owner top dollar. The land-owner in exchange probably paid a 6% commission which means the farm manager got 6 cents richer for every extra dollar he got out of me. Mr. Farm Manager knew the crop insurance system well. He had a small piece of ground coming out of **CRP (Conservation Reserve Program), a USDA program which I un-affectionately call "Constructing Rural Poverty", and cowboys call it the "Cow Replacement Program"**, because for ten years the land sits idle while the USDA pays the land-owner to do nothing. In fact, they almost always pay above our area's prevailing rental rates for that honor. An attorney from 5 or 6 counties away hired the farm manager to manage his land asset in this area. Seems the cedar trees needed to be controlled after 10 years of neglect in CRP, so they wanted it farmed for three years so they could re-enroll in CRP for another 10 years of growing cedar trees and Constructing Rural Poverty. Sometimes the government will even give back-to-back contracts for all of this….that's 20 years, unbelievable!

The farm manager told me the cash rent he desired and I declined, because I don't farm for crop insurance especially at my 55% coverage level. The manager thought he could get that rent out of someone because of well, "just the math". The county had a T-yield of 140 and 140 times 80% insurance equals 112 bushel guarantee times a spring price guarantee of $4.00 per bushel equals $448 gross revenue lock times about a one third relationship between gross and rent equals 147.84 an acre rent, but he'd give me a break at $145/A. A week or two later, after all others on his call list were smart enough to also decline, he called back to offer it to me for free, and being Irish I accepted. Apparently no one wanted to mess with a small patch full of cedars. The deal was, I had to clean up the cedars. So I did some sweat equity, well me and the kids and the bean head, but first I loosened the belt on the wobble box and then I bought another belt and some sickles and guards to replace the ones I broke during harvest. As for the kids, they were already enrolled in our farms' WFFP, the "Work For Food Program" and were happy to earn another hot prepared meal, especially that medium rare sirloin steak!

The next year he wanted $160/A, but I was on to this piece of crap soil now, even after 10 years of "organically" resting in CRP, it couldn't raise hell with a quart full of whiskey, not even the good blended 90 proof stuff! He talked me into meeting with him to look at another piece of totally abused soil, since he already had me on the hook. It was toward evening which I think was a strategic plan of his to avoid discovery. We traveled about 7 miles west in his rig. This was a bigger piece, maybe 200 acres but it was not coming out of CRP because it was already being farmed. We hadn't even walked across the gravel from where we parked before some "ole' boy" in his chore truck had sniffed us out and comes roaring up and angrily asked if we were the farm managers of this ground. Since I thought honesty might be the best policy here, I pointed to the Land Manager, after all, they get paid the big money. The chore truck farmer proceeded to give the Farm manager a tongue lashing about how deep the gullies were all across that farm from the years of shoddy farming practices. The chore truck man told him, "You don't care about the land, only the money." He also said that there was no way that farm should qualify for the first bit of government payments because it was clearly "out of compliance". Everything the chore truck guy said was true as I was soon to find out.

It was hard to walk around that piece of ground and not carry a bias, but soon I was working hard on not carrying a grudge. Gullies were so deep you would have to put end rows along them creating a bunch of little fields where a big field once was. Waterways needed to be established everywhere you looked. Missouri creek crossings needed to be improved to culvert crossings sometimes just to get the planter to clear the low point to a new patch. No money had been spent to improve this ground, it was a crop insurance farm. No soil tests were available so you can only assume it was "mined" of its fertility for at least the three years where the previous farmer was still benefiting from the county T-yield which crop insurance allows before the actual production history (APH) starts to really lower the revenue guarantee. I was a crop insurance adjuster for 5 years and I saw this three year then rotate to a "new producer" thing being used on a really poorly drained abused piece of land in another state, an example of gaming the system. Why is the system gamed....because it exists!

Maybe now is the time to point out a paradox in the USDA regarding soil conservation policy. I would hear it all the time, especially from the N.E. Iowa dairy farmers, "the government doesn't care about conservation, or else they'd have paid us to have more hay and pasture." Oh so true. Incentives and subsidies to keep land in hay or pasture were totally ignored for generations of farm programs and just recently received some love through insurability from crop insurance. The subsidies were all for corn/soy/wheat/oats in the midwest. Soil conservation, which is one of the main missions of the USDA's NRCS office takes a back seat to money distribution, control, and access to data....and whatever else. With all the black snow I've seen in the road ditches of the midwest during the winter of '23/'24, I think the taxpayers are still getting a very poor return on investment with the NRCS.

17.

Diversion: USDA's Ag Census - Jail Time.

The USDA has a serious information/data fetish. They get acre and crop data when farmers sign up for mainstream programs, then again with ad hoc programs, then again with crop insurance sign-up, then again from satellite imaging for crop reports, then again if they want to "fly" over, then again and most thoroughly in the USDA's N.A.S.S. (National Ag. Statistics Service) "Census of Agriculture".

CENSUS OF AGRICULTURE
National Agricultural Statistics Service
1201 E 10th St
Jeffersonville IN 47133
OFFICIAL BUSINESS
Penalty for Private Use $300
22-A7.2 (9-2021)

PRSRT STD
POSTAGE & FEES PAID
USDA
Permit No. G-38

FORWARDING SERVICE REQUESTED

USDA 2022 CENSUS OF AGRICULTURE
YOUR VOICE. YOUR FUTURE. YOUR OPPORTUNITY.

U.S. CENSUS OF AGRICULTURE REPORT ENCLOSED
YOUR RESPONSE IS REQUIRED BY LAW
Overdue: Return within 10 days

Who Should Report?
A reply is required from EVERYONE who receives a report form, including persons who operated a farm, ranch, or other agricultural operation in 2022, anyone who has any agricultural activity, as well as those who were not involved in agriculture. You may complete your report form online. Go to www.agcounts.usda.gov and enter your unique 12-digit survey code from the Census mailing label. More Census information is on the Internet at www.agcensus.usda.gov.

If you do not complete the form online or return your report form by mail, you will continue to receive contacts from us.

If you were a landlord only and rented out all your land, complete the front page, Section 1, and Section 36 on the back

Notice the warning "Your response is required by law" with the overdue statement in red. I want to thank my buddy for sharing this envelope with me.

Farmers and Ranchers get these threatening letters from the USDA asking us for farm production numbers. Only 24 pages worth! If you don't give them what they want, a goon may or may not show up at your door to collect the information, as they did with my buddy. It was an unannounced visit to the farm, and when his dad wasn't home to talk to the information collector, the kid was threatened with, "We'll be back." We are thinking the dutiful son matched the threatening attitude of the info collector, and the mutually disrespectful exchange ended with no more unwanted visits. We can't send a balanced budget through Congress, but the USDA can send information collecting goons hither and yon to find out how many tractors we are using; This data gathering has to be an FDR modeled "jobs works project". They should call it the WPA-WTM; We Piddle Around - With Taxpayers Money.

The cover letter to the 24 page info dump gives reference to a law which requires us to surrender our proprietary info to their Holiness. Title 7 USC 2204 (g) Public Law 105-113. Can you believe we have a law where private citizens must surrender their proprietary information so that a Secretary of some bureaucratic department can do as he wishes with it. Seriously, they don't own our farms, yet! I read the law so you would know, "Part B. Method. says; The Secretary may conduct any survey or other information collection, and employ any sampling or other statistical method, that the Secretary determines is appropriate". Part D. says; "Enforcement: 1.)Fraud or false information on any question is punishable w/up to $500 fine." 2.)Refusal to submit or answer is punishable w/up to $100 fine. All of the above gives the Secretary of Agriculture the power of a King.

Is a law like this in any industry other than Agriculture? Does Dodge have to report how many Minivans are on their sales lot vs. their manufacturing lot, and whether they are being used to haul kids vs. used to haul feed bags; I think not. Many-a "very bad" farmer has told his story about what he's done with these reports, and some of it has been more than a little disrespectful.

I also think some of those same rebel farmers are incorrectly using their Dodge feedvans to haul mini kids.

This Ag Census is a law that should be wiped off the books and the Census dealt with in a voluntary fashion or through communications with other intergovernmental agencies. Taxes are one thing we have to do, but this? Independent types like ranchers don't feel overly compelled to divulge all their proprietary information with any source, much less a non-essential government agency threatening fines. I see a lot of "civil disobedience" on this one and in a small way it helps define how far we can be pushed. Hopefully they will never put those "bad farmers" in jail and deny "due process rights." In our country of laws you are not supposed to be able to imprison a person and deny a speedy trial just because you don't agree with their politics. I've never seen our individual guaranteed liberties be so subject to a political litmus test as we see today. The pundits are now calling this lawfare. How divisive is this to a nation? We all fear that if the political persecution of Trump is successful, then we are next. This is not our good old USA if it continues. The answers are in the constitution, and I don't think there's any intent in that document to fine farmers who don't take a USDA survey. I say let the universities and private analysts do much of what the USDA N.A.S.S. is currently doing. A big problem with statistics being gathered and reported by governmental agencies is that no-one is accountable when the numbers are wrong, and wrong happens about every year in soybeans. If a private agency overestimates national soybean yield, the customer of that service can cease to do business with them.

Back to the conservation paradox that the USDA has had going on for years. The game my whole life was to maximize corn base at the USDA office in order to maximize payments, because that is the way the USDA set it up. So, more corn means less hay and pasture. I like corn, but growing it back-to-back requires more tillage, and more tillage means more chocolate color in the streams, which in turn means more nutrients like phosphorus moving toward the gulf of Mexico, which in turn means a lot of fisherman in the gulf burning more fossil fuel to get all the way out of the dead zone water to get to good fishing.

Like I said earlier, hay and especially pasture were left out of almost every farm commodity program. Now you see how government policy hurts soil conservation and has a negative effect on other industries. Maybe in another life I'll figure out more about the fishing/shrimping industry and exactly how they have adapted to the nutrient rich dead zone at the mouth of the Mississippi river as it dumps into the Gulf.

18.

Diversion: Cutting Nutrient Rates

A short topical story on conservation and shrimp, then I'll wrap up the story on the land rent.

Once upon a time 7 years ago I tried to help the shrimp and win a million dollar prize from a challenge offered up by Tulane University called the, "Million$ dead zone challenge". They were primarily interested in reducing Nitrogen dumping into the Gulf, it seemed like Phosphorus was getting a little disrespected in the challenge so I included it in my plan. My plan was really more of a "deal", but it was pretty simple, and it followed an existing model established successfully by the herbicide Atrazine. My proposed "Cut the Rate" deal offered that the agriculture and turfgrass industries self-regulate a maximum use rate on Nitrogen (140 units) and Phosphorus (70 units P205) in exchange for them backing off of over-regulation from the proposed "Waters-of-the-U.S." rules and threats of a Mississippi watershed TMDL (total maximum daily load) U.S. EPA enforcement policy. I think our industry would rather self-regulate than be told which land and in what watershed can and can't be farmed and we should keep industry wide self-regulation in mind in case regulators want to go all Chesapeake Bay (a more onerous water quality program) on the midwest. In the deal, the job of oversight would then be given to the states, Departments of Ag., just like with herbicides. This was not a voluntary plan I proposed. As long as the whole industry was required to adopt the maximum use rates nationwide, which are designed to keep yield w/in the 95th percentile the farmer would gross the same $/acre because laws of supply and demand would do their thing. Usually an 11 billion bushel crop is worth more than a 13 billion bushel sized U.S. corn crop. Most farmers wouldn't mind hauling less bushels around as long as it is worth more per bushel.

The "CUT THE RATE" deal

The Deal we propose: The Agriculture and Turf-grass industries "self-regulate" into law the following maximum use rates of Nitrogen and Phosphorus (2017-'27) to save ourselves from two eminent problems:

1. Over-regulation from the U.S. EPA and the Clean Water Act.
2. Over-production

In exchange we get a 10 year deal of continuing exemption from the Clean Water Act/WOTUS/TMDL's.

140 units actual N/A/yr. (applied inorganic and/or available organic forms)

70 units actual P2O5/A/yr. (")

Model program: Atrazine 2lb/A BMP laws. Designated special use areas more restrictive.

Enforcement: State Departments of Agriculture, like atrazine.

Scope: All acres of grain and oilseed and turf-grass in the U.S.A.

Goal: 20% reduction in nitrogen and phosphorus discharge into the waters of the U.S. without adversely affecting the livelihood of farmers.

Intended Result: Return profitability and accountability to the farm without the federal government inserting another bureaucracy into our industry without meaningful results. Reduce taxpayer and check-off dollars used on this problem. Help a future generation of farmers learn how to do better with less.

The following graphs are from Nitrogen research looking at N rates on yield and tile drainage N concentration. Nitrogen might be the most over researched thing ever in farming. I included this "graph" evidence to win the water prize. I also sent all this info to the Iowa Department of Agriculture encouraging them to take the lead on industry self-regulation. They said a voluntary nutrient reduction system was the way to go instead.

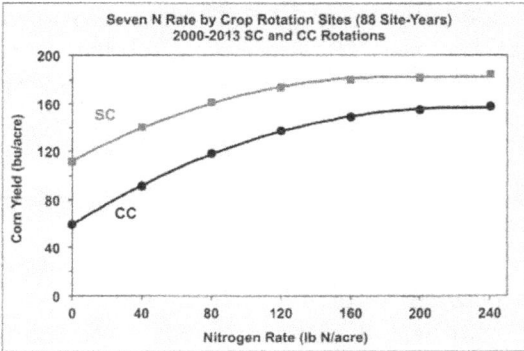

Figure 1. Yield of corn in continuous corn (CC) and corn following soybean (SC) across time with multiple rates of actual N fertilizer applied (Sawyer and Barker, 2013, Iowa State University).

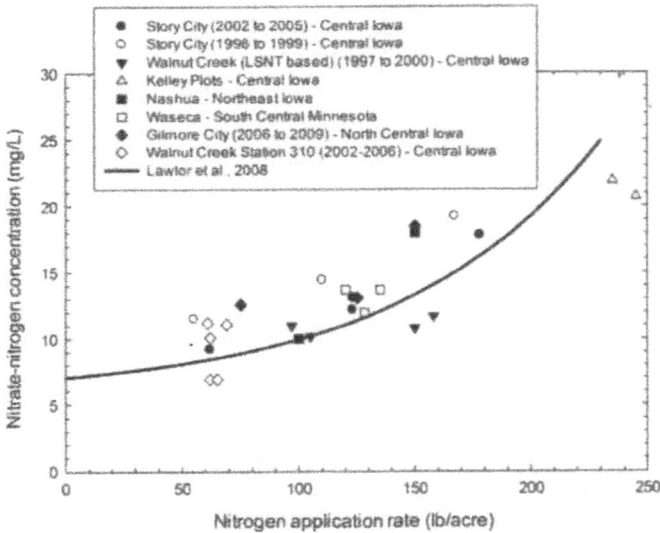

Figure 1. Nitrogen application rate effect from various studies on tile drainage nitrate-N concentration for a corn-soybean rotation compared to the tile-flow response curve developed by Lawlor et al. (2008).

I wasn't advocating for a "voluntary nutrient reduction strategy (VNRS)" like Iowa currently has, I'm talking real maximum use rates like Atrazine has. The problem with a voluntary system is that no one volunteers. It defies economic logic for me to cut my nitrogen rate and reduce my yield when no one else in the watershed or for that matter the whole country is doing it. The designers of the voluntary plans had to know about that fundamental flaw, but maybe they just had to have a plan, any plan to make it look like we were doing something, and we are, but at a very snail-like pace. One thing that amazes me about the VNRS is that they are very successful at harvesting money for research and grants, but not so much progress on cleaning up lakes and streams. They have received so much money it's hard for them to find enough farmer cooperators to take the free money. Results of our VNRS are often measured in dollars harvested and not in nutrient loads reduced.

Please realize my ulterior motive here. From a farmers perspective anything that lowers our overproduction "nationally", also raises price. I feel confident that good land and good management can hold onto 95% of former yields and that the price will more than compensate for yield. On any of the three areas of the midwest I have farmed, I would split my 140 units into 40 units with the planter and 100 units sideress and all my corn would be on a rotation with legumes like soybeans.

You ask, "How do you keep a farmer from putting her normal 200 unit rate on?" Well, you probably don't at first. Just like Atrazine, when we put a 2 lb./Acre (1.5 lb in some karst topographies) limit on it, it became part of our culture and the farmers who were defiant just had to eventually learn to do with less, because the suppliers weren't going to be enablers. I was around the herbicide industry a lot when atrazine relabeled and never knew a soul to get fined and within a few years I never knew a soul to abuse the label. Then, as a result of our rate cuts we heard less about atrazine problems in our water reservoirs. A simple solution and a real success story. Now a lot of the corn acres have even gravitated toward suitable alternatives to Atrazine.

Livestock medications have maximum dosages, herbicides,

insecticides, fungicides and biological amendments all have very specific dosage rates on their labels. I've often wondered how everything we use on the farm has a maximum use rate except our two biggest environmental problems: Nitrogen and Phosphorus. Can you imagine the innovation that would develop the minute we had a maximum use rate on Nitrogen! Suddenly all the "soil health" promotion and research becomes relevant. Unlocking new innovations in efficiency and conservation and soil health, or finding hybrids that can scavenge for nitrogen wouldn't be a bad result, would it? I'll bet we could even pick up some more customers overseas.

I also included the turfgrass industry in this "cut the rate deal." It perplexes farmers why suburbanites go to such effort to nutrify a lawn so that they get to mow it more often. I'm not saying one shouldn't take pride in their homestead, but I think the same maximum use rates should also apply to lawns.

Needless to say, I did not win the challenge money or else I'd be on some beach somewhere! I should get better at remembering rejection, but I think they said, "We are not interested in regulating midwest farmers." Seems like Tulane U. wanted a contraption to denitrify water as it dumped into the Gulf, guess that's why they called it a challenge because the river at New Orleans is *only* a half mile wide and 200 ft. deep.

You are dying to know who won the prize. The winner is a professional software tool for agronomists to manage nitrogen recommendations, integrating 13 different models for simplicity. I won't mention the name because after 7 years I still haven't heard of it being used in our industry. I did notice it was developed at Cornell University. I saw monkeys doing this once at the zoo, "I'll scratch your back if you'll scratch mine," but sometimes even that deal breaks down and then the monkeys start slinging dung at each other. I'm not bitter about losing or anything.

Obviously if there is a million dollar prize available for a solution, there must be a problem. Multiple ideas get floated around, from a virtual outlaw of fall tillage and fall fertilizing, to a requirement for cover crops on all tillable acres. One proposal I find most interesting came from a group in Ohio who were also bothered that farmers in flat land country had no obligations to conservation compliance unlike farmers in Highly Erodible Land (HEL) country, yet flatlanders seemed to be as much or more the problem for nutrient and soil loss. The solution they proposed is that all farmers receiving government subsidies be required to put buffer strips around all water conveyance or water holding landforms. I'm thinking they proposed 30 foot hay buffers so that hay could be harvested. Why should HEL land be the only land with conservation requirements they ask? On our farm we use these types of hay buffers in many places and pictured is one near our fishing pond shown doing its job. As you can see, hay buffers manage to catch a lot of the spring fertilizer runoff (see the darker hay being nutrified by fertilizer movement off of our unplanted soybean stubble no-till field). The hay caught the nutrients and the fish thrive in the pond and the taxpayer doesn't have to pay for any of this.

19.

Back to the Crop Insurance Farm

The big land rental deal: had there been no government programs, the farm I was looking at would have still been in pasture, I'm quite certain of that. Reflecting on the chore truck guy's comment about the farm being out of compliance, which theoretically waives your right to any USDA payment. The price he was asking for the farm did not reflect all the work or money it would require to fix it, it only reflected the math created by a government subsidized crop insurance system, $160/A. I thought I had some leverage here because if this farm is officially declared out of compliance the next farmer will have to buy expensive unsubsidized crop insurance and I've been buying that for years.

Since I have a conscience, I would have to improve this farm so my bid had to reflect the costs I would incur to do so. My bulldozer would have to do "primary tillage" on a farm I was going to no-till. My generous bid was $120/acre and a commitment to fix gullies and water crossings over a multiyear contract. After two weeks I was thankfully rejected. As I have since learned on these abused farms there is very little topsoil left, and very little hope for decent yields, and the farm becomes very dependent on crop insurance. In only one generation a conventional tilled shallow soil type rolling farm can lose all of its black top soil and offer up only yellow clay, where corn only grows a nubbin, that's if you can get it to emerge. All the genetics in the world can't make up for ruined soil.

20.

Conservation Problems Caused by Government Programs

Ironically, CRP has taken a terrible toll on soil conservation in our neighborhood – hang in there with me. A tremendous amount of land has been converted from its more native use of pasture and hay only to be tilled and farmed for three years so that it can qualify to be enrolled in "10 year" as it is often called. Conservation Reserve Program (CRP) is a ten year idle acre, golden parachute retiree program designed and controlled by the USDA and funded by taxpayers. Did I mention it idles acres for ten years and pays the landowner to do nothing! In theory it could be very good at holding soil once the stand of native grasses or wildflowers or warm season prairie grass gets established, the problem is getting to that point. It may take 5 years of soil erosion to get 10 years of CRP, first the three years of taking it out of its native use to meet the 3 year row crop requirement. Then at least a year to really cover the soil especially when seeding to a warm season prairie grass or wildflowers, then it is usually tilled multiple passes when it is released from CRP to get rid of anthills or gopher mounds or gullies, yes I said gullies and serious ones too. Do not go speeding across a CRP field chasing a wild animal on your four wheeler or motor bike unless you want to end up like a kid of mine with two broken wrists and many different versions of a bad story to tell Dad. If you are a dad with that kind of kid who always has to gear things up a notch, consider trading the motorbike in for something safer, like a Chevette maybe. If you can't bring yourself to get rid of the motor bike, go out and buy a short statured used pine sawhorse, drape some shop rags over it, clamping them from the bottom of the 2 x 6 beam and tell your enthusiastic youngster, "if you break both of your wrists, it's just you and this sawhorse when it comes to the toilet." Why is it that most of the lasting lessons in life involve pain?

To add insult to injury, once the CRP gets well established the big burn happens. Yup, instead of letting all of the photosynthesis derived carbon cycle into the soil, huge government endorsed and financed "controlled" burns spew all accumulated biomass into the atmosphere resulting in a smoky haze over our area for days in the early spring. In 2023 a big nature conservancy with land to our south had such a big burn it formed a condensation cloud over top of the burn, probably altering weather cycles on the planet for decades, okay maybe centuries. How do you like that, "Green New Dealers" and conservancy investors! Occasionally these burns "get away" and mow down a neighbor's CRP and nearby barns, three generations of pickup trucks and all, something our already understaffed local fire departments cannot afford to battle, also ruining our daily drivers.

Government rental rates have also been a problem with CRP. The CRP bids would occasionally hit $260/acre. Yes, the USDA outbids the normal row crop operation by $100, cattlemen by $200/acre, often times giving that money to an absentee landowner who then calls his buddy and says, "buy some of that rough ground in southern Iowa to hunt deer on, put it in CRP the government will make your payment, don't rent it to a local, they won't pay near what the government will, and it's a 10 year guaranteed deal, you don't have to do a thing and you can hunt all over it." In some years the USDA has also offered an "up front bonus" to get more land in the program! So all of a sudden the local farmer and especially the cow/calf operation who can maybe muster $80 for pasture is run right out of competing for land, thanks to an artificial economy created by the government. Now you see why I call CRP, "constructing rural poverty".

Hold onto your hat again. While signing our Ohio land up for the CAUV (certified Ag use valuation)program which basically verifies that its use is farm land and not development land, therefore giving farmers a cheaper land tax rate than developers, as they should. The county for which I was signing had a notice that you had to update CRP contract information or potentially lose your *tax break for CRP*. This sent my B.S. detect-o-meter bouncing off the stops. Can you believe the Ohio legislature takes money away from the county for land enrolled in the USDA's CRP program? A call to the county assessor confirmed this and the fellow on the other end of the line said they were very upset at the legislature and the big Farm lobbyist for pushing this through. With an aggressive push to enroll even more acres into CRP in Ohio at rental rates of $500 to $1500/A, how is the farmer going to compete with the USDA? How is the county infrastructure going to compete with the USDA? Why would the big farm lobbyists be involved in trying to construct more rural poverty? What possible rationale could there be to give an acre of golden parachute ground a tax break vs. the acre right next to it that's doing a capital generating function? Where's that straightjacket?

I wish there was a bigger movement afoot amongst farmers and farm groups to ask that **CRP rental rates be limited to "no more than the county average pasture rental rates", which would be $85/A for our county.** I know any farm group that has let me attend a meeting will hear this proposal. This solution would prevent them from running cattlemen out of business. That is the best proposal I see short of ending it right here/right now. Ending it all together would be best for the longevity of our rural communities because the young farmers can't rent land if the government already has it rented.

In a real twist of fate for the farmers living in CRP rich areas, ironically or moronically the Iowa Department of Natural Resources prohibits those same absentee landowners, if they are out-of-staters, from getting a deer hunting license annually. It is not uncommon to have 10%-20% of our crop eaten by the huge mismanaged deer herd with ever shrinking antler size.

The DNR says they are properly managing our deer herd based on their data, so I had to ask what counts contribute to their data, because the masses are not asses and we locals are all having trouble with this massive herd. Right away I found a problem. They use deer/vehicle collisions to help determine herd size. Note to DNR folks in all states, please throw out your deer/vehicle collision data. People who live out here in rural America adapt to our environment. We have adapted to the huge deer herd by not turning in "hits" to our insurance because we cannot afford comprehensive insurance, much less pay deductibles for every collision. We drive beaters with nothing but liability insurance. As an example, the old Impala has endured 5 such collisions with no claim ever, just a lot of new front headlights. The people who don't drive old beaters often use bumper guards and just mow them down and never report. The poor people around here who drive nice vehicles with no bumper guards I feel sorry for, please slow down for the love of God, slow down for your own safety! A southern Iowa driver's license shouldn't be a deer hunting license. Farms have to carry all this liability insurance for our livestock but the DNR has no liability. I'm tired of seeing those vigil crosses along the road, some of which I personally know are from deer hits. A motorcycle is even higher risk and a deer-motorcycle accident almost cost a friend of mine and his wife their lives, in broad daylight.

We need the DNR to give a deer hunting license to all out-of-staters, charge them plenty, but make them "earn-a-buck" by harvesting two doe's before they are issued a buck tag.... our vehicles will thank you too! Other states have done this. Now there's something big farm lobbying groups who own auto insurance companies can lobby for more deer harvested by hunters, not automobiles. Then they could offer lower auto insurance premiums! I just had a win/win idea.

Next, I will give a classic example of unintended consequences resulting from the CRP program. You know how the road to hell is paved with good intentions. Let us say Farmer Jill looks at hay as a cash flow crop. She decides to put a crop of hay in her more erosion prone fields or just leave an established field of meadow hay because it is rough and erodible. She cash flows this idea to the banker valuing the hay at $70/bale. The farm lobby comes along and says, "there is a shortage of hay this year (maybe because all those acres are in CRP)," then they make a successful plea to state USDA officials to release CRP acres to make hay off of. Suddenly Jill's $70 hay is competing with hoards of $40 hay sold cheap because it essentially gets "stolen" from the taxpayer who thought they were investing in conservation when in reality they were investing in a "Buffering Supply (B.S.)" program for hay. All of this backdoor activity lowers the hay market and prevents Farmer Jill from achieving her price objective and the banker is not happy and says, "we may have to go back to co-signed checks," unless of course you go ahead and put a program crop like corn or soybeans on that land. Farmer Jill is not happy either. Soil conservation goes backwards again because now she is going to get out of hay and go to a program crop of corn or soy.

The 30 by 30 government initiative should probably be mentioned here. Its goal is 30% of land and water will be "protected or conserved" by 2030, following a far reaching international agenda. This is a Biden administration plan announced in Jan. 2021, through executive order 14008, with the feel-good title "America the Beautiful Initiative". In April of '22 there was a "Stop 30x30 Summit held in Omaha Nebraska by folks who questioned the acts motives. The argument made at that summit was, "30x30 is an unconstitutional policy shift, moving us from a nation founded on private property principles to one controlled by the administrative state." Do the above mentioned CRP acres contribute to the goal, who knows?

Rural areas fear that to accomplish 30 x 30 goals, more land will be sold to "tax exempt" groups, pulling much needed tax base away from fire, police, schools, county government, and hospitals. In plains states land tracts with conservation easements and associated tax abatements are causing counties to consider dissolution.

In a move related or not to 30 x 30, the S.E.C. has been asked to list Natural Asset Companies (NACs) on the New York Stock

Exchange creating accounts to trade in "management of the nation's conservation assets" It seemed like an invitation for foreign investors to tip-toe through our tulips, here in the USA. Can you imagine giving management rights and an easement in perpetuity to a country who wishes ill will. Thankfully, Iowa and Nebraska Senators stopped it, at least for now. For national security reasons, foreign ownership of USA natural resource assets should be stopped. We also need to take that "policing" job away from the USDA and give it to someone with a badge and a gun. Any foreign control of our land or food is a huge national security threat and should be taken way more seriously.

The great irony of all this conservation/CRP/30x30 activity is that it is designed, or at least sold to the American people, as a way to gain urbanites and suburbanites access to green space/ outdoor recreation and preservation of endangered species, and maybe carbon sinks. If it is carbon sequestration they want, they should accept our no-till acres of corn/soy/wheat to contribute to their theoretical numbers. Meanwhile they go about trying to create a new endangered species, the rural American, driving us out of our rural lands and into a city so that we need the "recreation space" they now control (through easements) in the country. Can someone please help us defund these kind of onerous programs from our federal government! Why is the USDA complicit in any of these rural depopulation endeavors? A quick search of the net reveals a 5% decline in rural population from 2010 to 2020 and expects another 5% decline '20 to '30.

21.

The HFSA and its Relationship to the "179"

To get back on track with the HFSA, not only does it hybridize the Health Savings Account (HSA) concept but also the **"179", which is probably the most popular tax play ever for farmers and businesses in the years when money is made.** It's basically a form of accelerated depreciation. For example, instead of taking 7 years to depreciate a tractor, using the "179" you can do it all in one year. Farmers like machines and are always needing or at least wanting to update, so they often use this "179" tax play to reduce taxable income and improve their machinery lineups. The downside is they lose the ability to depreciate that piece of equipment in later years. Another downside to using the "179" is that machines are not a good reservoir for money because if you use them, they devalue, then they devalue even more if your kids use them. Of course there are limitations on how many dollars are eligible and what equipment buildings or pickup trucks qualify. At the end of the year, if the tax person gives the green light, "it's go time" and the checks start flying! The tax people know this is good for the economy. Consult with your tax advisor.

All I'm asking for is tax law which allows farmers using the

HFSA access to one half of the qualifying "179" distribution. The equipment sellers will still get at least 50% and our local banks will get some serious tax preferred accounts designed to help farmers help themselves. The money in the HFSA account must be liquid and accessible without penalty. The money should be taxed at the tax rate of the year it is pulled out of the account, unless funds could be qualified for a tax-free withdrawal because of a governor declared "emergency area" or approved "soil wellness" investment. I see the value this account may have for income averaging and securing or leveraging operating capital. The banks should not be allowed to get this money held in an account at checking account rates, which are a joke. The banks should be required to pay an interest rate which is related to something like the prime lending rate, 10 year treasury notes, or Fed. reserve bond market rates or LIBOR. Let's say the banks could work for about a 3% cut, the prime lending rate which is currently about 8%, means the HFSA in 2023 should yield the farmer about 5% interest. Using the old bankers rules of 3:6:3, where bankers pay depositors 3%, charge borrowers 6%, and hit the golf course by 3 o'clock.... we can get to at least 5% for the HFSA, any less and golf courses will be full of bankers by noon. I happen to know a Nebraska banker who could use all that extra time, and still not fix his broken golf game!

Wouldn't it be great to get a Land Grant to take on the task of helping us design such an account. They have all the right tools, knowledge, even experience. I could really use their input on how to determine maximum withdrawals from the account, should they be limited to the amount of farm loss on schedule 1040F when using the tax-free option triggered by a "disaster area" declaration. My interaction with one of the Land Grant institutions yielded nothing but head scratching. When asking their help, just as Sen. Grassley's aid had requested, I was told via voice mail, "Our department's mission is to evaluate, not to promote an idea, so no, we would not be able to work with you on this HFSA concept." He might as well said, "Endeavor to persevere!"

I ask, where does evaluation end and promotion begin? For example, a professor may be a consultant who in addition to his

University job helps to design a value added product for crop insurance. Let's call the product "revenue protection plus." Articles are published, seminars are conducted by this professor to then explain to farmers all of the new options crop insurance offers and how new options can be used to insure profitability. Promotion or evaluation, which is it? Seems like a fine line. I would rather they had said, "Your idea is terrible and here's why.......!" I would really like them to say, "We have a better idea, one that advances our mission statement of enriching rural communities while not leveraging your kids' future. Would you like to provide input from the field?" My reply of course would be, "Yes, and since I am out standing in my field, let me get out of the wind first...." Gratuitous farmer joke.

Some interest in the HFSA has been shown by a western Land Grant University who was trying to address market inequities encountered as a result of crop insurance use and abuse. I tried to sell this University on the advantage an HSFA may have for putting an end to market distorting practices like revenue protection crop insurance, encouraging them to consider tying the HFSA to a more catastrophic version of bushel type crop insurance. I tried to get them to consider the advantages this HFSA gives to a beginning farmer or the livestock farmer/rancher. Independent livestock has generally been left out of most mainstream USDA programs, why shouldn't livestock in the least get the HFSA. I sent my outline, I even called back, reminded me of my days trying to get a date....cricket, cricket.

22.

Crop Insurance Reforms Needed

A s of now, I'm thinking the above-mentioned University has decided to look more into crop insurance reforms, which I can agree also needs to be done. They should start with reforming Actual Production History (APH). First, end the 5% reporting allowance for APH, it gets a lot of abuse. Next, a new farming entity should get stuck with the yield history of the field they are farming, just like the name APH implies. A much abused loophole is that new farmers get a new t-yield (or county average yield), that needs to end. Also, multiple counties should not be able to function as if they are separate "units", unless the farmer pays for the more expensive optional unit purchase price, hence putting an end to bushel shuffling between counties. Also, enforcement of soil conservation rules should "actually happen" (not just be selectively applied to people they don't like) which would in turn kick violators into the unsubsidized category, as laid out in the 1985 farm bill. Also, the FSA offices should not be willing accomplices to organizing farms that are under one management into multiple entities. Aunt Martha might be a nice lady with a unique social security number, but if she isn't buying her own seed corn, chemicals, fertilizer, parts, fuel, more parts, tires, parts, oils, parts, oh and grinding a few gears; she is probably not "actively engaged."

I think "parts" might need to be the new barometer for being actively engaged in farming. Also, R.A. (revenue assurance) should not exist, only bushel insurance, putting an end to paying farmers with high APH's on a year when they still have big yields. As an adjuster, in the 2008 time frame I remember paying a claim to a farmer who had a great yield of 178 bu/a corn, all because of revenue assurance (R.A.). This R.A. policy would probably price itself out of existence in an unsubsidized environment. Eventually subsidies to crop insurance should be pulled and farmers should shoulder the entire cost, just as they do with hail insurance. Do you know why Hail Insurance adjusters always get the short end of the stick? Because the long end got hailed off! Adjuster joke, man I miss those parties.

I must admit, even in my own farming operation when I was buying the higher rate insurances of 70+% coverage levels, there was a tendency to "swing for the fence" on yield. We all strive for a big APH because 70% of 200 bu./A is a higher guarantee than 70% of 150 bu./A, it's the math. None of this is lost on the farmer and since crop insurance is the elephant in the room, it has tweaked our assessment of "the point of diminishing return." We seed corn at higher rates even on this droughty land to be offensive because the defensive strategy has become insurance rather than low plant populations. I will also argue the push for ever higher APH's has resulted in more tillage to get that soil warmed up quicker and increase the chance of pulling that extra 15 bu./A in corn, instead of a defensive strategy like no-till. It has also resulted in those extra units of nitrogen and phosphorus and potassium applied to ensure that none of these elements limit yield. Nitrogen especially. Is anyone using less than 200 total units of Nitrogen/A anymore? (the "cut the rate deal" would take us to 140 total units~95th percentile on yield.) You now see another example of how a government subsidized economic system can be detrimental to the environment, because of the added incentive for yield.

23.

HFSA: How It Can Help the Next Generation of Farmers

As for the young people wanting to get into farming or ranching let's help them help themselves by allowing up to $20,000 before tax income be put into an HFSA account. Since I propose access to the HFSA is thru IRS form 1040F (Farm), that means somehow young people have to claw their way into at least some farm involvement, maybe serious backyard chickens since eggs are $6.00/dozen (2023). It takes $1000 of gross sales for the USDA to consider you a farmer, IRS definitions are more vague and I was unsuccessful in finding a minimum requirement to access form 1040 schedule F. Unfortunately I know losses can be filed on this form, told you the cow/calf business is rough, and if you don't believe me ask that lady named Beth on the Yellowstone T.V. series. Go ahead ask Beth, if you got the guts! Oh wait, that's fiction.

I've heard many Ag economists address the age problem we have in farming where the average age in our profession is 60 years. How does that young guy buy out the 60 year old retiring farmer with chicken egg money? It would take 2833 dozen to buy an acre of ground in our old neighborhood of Dubuque County ($17,000/A land). This is a very real problem. The popular Land Grant solution to this problem is to give that kid a long term USDA guaranteed loan for 2 or 3% under prevailing interest rates so that kid can be a serf to the USDA for the next 30 years. Another paradox. It's not as much an interest problem as it is a principle problem, and the principle problem is created by USDA programs that have inflated land values, programs like CRP, crop insurance, USDA grants for wind and solar. For the Land Grants U's, we again get to that fine line between promotion vs. evaluation, wouldn't they serve our rural communities better by promoting a different path than the current USDA design. The current path is crushing our kids' opportunities to farm. Wouldn't it be better to let the kid take some of his off farm income and build real equity for a while with an off farm job, stick it in an HFSA and build capital. After all, capital, not eggs, is what it's going to take to get into farming. Some kids are making serious money in their two income families and they aren't pumping out as many Cheerios eating tax write-offs anymore, they are getting pounded on income tax, let them have a tax break or at least a tax deferment, "for the love of God!" There's Chris Farley when you need him.

I feel compelled to mention what a bad investment farmland looks like right now for a young family, because of its poor cash flow ability. The quick math for farmers evaluating land cash flow can be looked at in either of two ways. Simply consider the purchase as if it's an investment where you throw no equity at it and it has to carry its own weight on interest alone. Using an 8% interest rate, and an Iowa farmland average price for '23 @ $12,000/acre, equals an annual payment of $960/A on interest only, without even touching the principle yet. Let's say you rent it out at Iowa's average cash rent of $270/A, leaving a deficit of $690/A on interest alone, really bad for cash flow unless you desire cash to flow out. Not a good option for young families. Not even a good investment at 3% interest. It used to be that farmland required ⅓ down, but now banks tend to require significantly more down payment to make an amortization schedule cash flow. Now let's look at land investment from the other side as an investor who has cash to purchase farmland outright, $12,000/A which gets $270/A cash rent equals a 2%

R.O.I (return on investment) after real estate taxes. In comparison, the stock market long term average is 7 to 10% annualized R.O.I, depending on the web site. Also for a reference point, according to Investopedia the best 10 year CD (certificate of deposit) rate is 4%, doubling the return of land. So even from this second perspective farmland at current values looks like a bad investment, unless you are quite certain of an increase or appreciation in land values. Long term land usually looks like a good investment but a trough can last for 10 years. Either way you look at it, buying farmland right now and for most of my life has been a rich man's sport.

Not to discourage any youngster from getting into farming, but you must be realistic. Commodities are commodities and growing them usually results in narrow margins of $50 to $150 per acre (maybe even negative). Pick your time to get into a farmland investment, land prices cycle and bubbles burst, always have. An older house and buildings on a farm sometimes come for almost free, but don't pay too much for them because the last owner's liability may become yours. Opportunities to purchase land that provides positive cash flow are rare and may only come around twice in a lifetime, so save some money and be ready. Prove yourself to be a worker and never be afraid to make an offer that works for you. No is not always forever.

You are correct if you would argue land purchase should not be an approved use of the HFSA account tax free, but the money in the HFSA could be used as an asset to leverage future borrowing or to provide for future troubles, there is always that option to take money out and pay taxes as if it was ordinary income. Going farther down the groundhog hole, a soil wellness inclusion could be built in just like they have built in wellness exams as covered procedures in our HSA/High Deductible health insurance policies. I would suggest cover crop seed costs or buffer strip seed costs be available to be pulled out of this account tax free, and no, I do not sell cover crop or buffer strip seed, just brake parts.

Finally on the HFSA I will say, never should money paid out of an FSA office qualify to go directly and untaxed into an HFSA account. When addressing this topic at a Farm Bureau

D. C. Savage

meeting in cow/calf county I asked for input from my peers, an opinion on whether or not contributions to the HFSA should be allowed from farm program monies, a quick witted lady immediately said; "hell no, we have no farm programs, only the grain guys do." My question was originally spawned from a conversation I had earlier on a national farm radio talk show in which a prominent D.C. policy advisor who was a guest on the show advised that I push the HFSA concept in that direction. I'm going to go with the lady wearing chaps on this one. No circulation of FSA money to an HFSA account, because it further leaves out those commodities and ranchers left out all along.

24.

Farm Radio, Lyme Disease, and Mice

Radio talk shows help us get through some of those long days in a tractor cab. A local favorite everywhere is Radio Tradio, where you can buy out a guy's whole fishing gear assortment of well-organized tackle boxes, poles, bait pails, dip net, stringers, all for only $100 from that frustrated wife of a guy who spent too much time at the 'ole lake. I had a moment of guilt once when I responded to a call from a lady selling this exact assortment of fishing equipment. When I arrived at the address she gave me, I couldn't believe how much nice stuff this gal was liquidating for $100. I was tempted to offer her more money, then I got to thinking about all the future lawyer bills I might be saving the poor husband or boyfriend, made me feel a little less guilty.

A.M. radio is not dead out here, nor is FM for that matter. There is nothing better than an old Eddie Rabbit song on AM's slightly washed out band waves. "OOO I'm drivin' my life away, search'n for a better way......" I use AM radio to check my electric fences for spark as you can hear that static pulse through the radio, beats the heck out of the ass-kicking you get when you tell your buddy to go out and take a leak on the wire, reassuring him it won't hurt as you choke down that laugh, just before he makes you choke down your teeth! (PSA-Public Service Announcement, the aforementioned practice may or may not cause sterility.) Was it worth it? Yeah, you don't even have to get out of the pickup to check wire, just pull up within a couple of feet and you should hear that static snap in the speakers. I have not tried this technique in every county or with every AM radio station in America (it's on my bucket list), so please do not just jump out and grab the wire with both hands if the AM radio does not static pulse. Some of those 1 plus joule low impedance fencers will make you wonder how you lived through their vicious hits. The arms feel like you got frogged by George Foreman, that vein on the left side of your neck throbs, and your heart tells you, "I can only take so much of this stuff." What kind of deranged human would even create such a beast? One joule seems to train all my cattle and then as low as .15 joules will hold them once they are trained, but don't ask the neighbors to confirm this, they still don't believe any cow could jump like Zucchini.

I like listening to farm radio so I can hear the farm markets tank every time the USDA releases another report, kind of like they are holding a voodoo doll in their grasp and needle 10s of thousands of farmers over the airwaves with their best guess inaccuracies. We all love their over-estimates of soybean yield and the "feed and residual use" slop pen they can go to make corn numbers work for them, not! Both AM and FM stations are doing a good job of providing both grain markets and death notices; here in 2024 it seems the two are indiscernible.

I don't have very many modern vehicles but has anyone else noticed the AM receivers they put in radios now are junk? A buddy of mine swears this is a conspiracy to keep us from hearing all sides of the debate. "They" wouldn't do that!

Sometimes I listen to farm talk radio on both AM and FM waves and I do appreciate that they are still O.K. with dissenting, non-status quo opinions, but they are rarely challenged. NPR (National Public Radio) on the other hand, is intolerant of dissenting opinions! We have an NPR station affiliated with our local university, so when I get in the combine, the only station I can get is NPR. The radio is the last priority of fixing that old heap is going to get, kind of like replacing a light bulb on the Titanic as it is listing to starboard. OK, truth be known this affliction is not isolated to only the combine. What I'm getting at here is that I listen to NPR more than I want! They have the most powerful signal and/or the most plentiful radio towers in the area.

Over the last 12 years I've made 4 attempts to call-in to NPR talk shows and the only attempt that landed me on the radio is when I called them "back" to criticize Trump for spending too much money on farm bailouts, as he truly did. They had not been able to get to me for my original topical argument, which I might add was contrary to their opinion. Yes, they have an opinion! This challenged me to test my theory that they do not want to hear dissenting opinion, so I stretched their next topic to where I could criticize Trump, gave them a different name & town, maybe Earl from Earlville, then I promptly dissed Trump and his funding of "everything USDA" to the call screener and boom, into the queue I went. A few minutes later I got to make my argument on radio. A successful test of my theory. If you think NPR is objective, I got a good fresh combine with a great radio to sell you!

May I present further evidence of NPR's lacking objectivity. This time coming from a prominent NPR editor Uri Berliner who wrote this in his critical essay about the company(taken from an A.P. article April 17,2024) "There's an unspoken consensus about the stories we should pursue and how they should be framed," he wrote. "It's frictionless-one story after another about instances of racism, transphobia, signs of the climate apocalypse, Israel doing something bad and the dire threat of Republican policies. It's almost like an assembly line." According to the article Berliner also said, "NPR is dominated by liberals and no longer has an open-minded spirit. He traced the change to coverage of Trump's presidency." For all of this honesty Berliner was rewarded with a suspension by NPR and soon after he resigned. He did however stop short of asking to defund public investment.

Radio is a wonderful thing to have on those long days with no other human interaction. Tractor cabs are awesome, but 1000 hours a year in a cab just listening to that diesel motor drone could result in less brain activity. Music all day makes my mind go mushy, but occasionally it helps on a day where tension rules. Generally, talk radio helps me pass the hours best. I think it is a shame our most powerful free signal in talk radio is coming from towers and transmitters bought with public funds but devoted to biased propaganda, attempting to prejudice listeners with divisive words like "misinformation" and "disinformation". Attempts to pull public money away from NPR have never worked, so let me suggest another way around this problem. Share the allotment of public money with the other side. Create a Rural National Public Radio(RNPR). Call it equal time, call it equity radio, call it exciting to think about the new opportunities. Perhaps some of the programming could overlap, like Click and Clack, the Tappet Bros. reincarnated. Great idea aye!

Now for a public service announcement about dealing with Lyme disease. I am not a doctor, even though the USDA guy calls me one. Part of my medical curiosity stems from having personally dealt with a weird disease called Lyme, some doctors don't even believe in it. So when you get it, you become your own doctor. Welcome to rural America's deer tick epicenter, southern Iowa. Lyme disease gets started with a tick bite from an infected deer tick only the size of a fine point ink pen mark on your skin, progresses to a raised bullseye lesion then starts to itch and make you drag down, it does about everything to your body except make you wear drag. "Inflammation nation" I call it. Achy joints, hazy brain, noodle legs, tingling feet, shortness of breath, and your get up and go just got up and went. Those tick injected spirochetes aren't very well understood by medicine, that's probably why doctors might have a tendency to blow this disease off.

On my first tick bite with the associated bullseye skin reaction, eventually I could tell my body was having trouble with it, so the Doctor prescribed doxycycline antibiotic, and by the halfway point in the prescription I went from zero to 100 on the get up and go meter. I don't know what else that antibiotic took care of in my body but it was hugely successful for a little while, but that overwhelming exhaustion would naggingly come back, especially after pulling another deer tick off. I started researching it more and found I had to use Vitamin B-12, I called it my TFP (Tough freaker pill), it really helped. Also, when my body and more specifically my feet started to feel dead, I would first look down to make sure they were still there, then I would take another round of antibiotics, this time minocycline, always within 5 days I would go from pooper man to superman. Then I found another accidental revelation, this lymes group deep down in the web said an antihistamine helped, so I tried over-the-counter Claritin and it did help, by this time I'm a couple of years into this crappy disease, fighting but not totally winning! I'm not looking for sympathy here, because I already know where I can find that!

I kept battling, using those three tools; antibiotics occasionally, B-12 and Claritin. Finally, I got very, very sick. This gut ache came along that no antacid or even chocolate milk could touch, I thought maybe it was an ulcer, but I try to live without stress. It steadily grew through calving season, into planting season, into spraying season, but not quite into haying season because by haying season I would have died, I think quite literally. I had gangrene in the lining of my gallbladder. I now know why they call it gangrene, because my brother who was working with me the day before I tapped out said I looked green. I said it might be from the grass I'd been eating to settle my gut, but not even grass would help, so the dogs got that one wrong. Nothing would stay down, not the grass, not the orange juice, I even thought my internal organs were going to come out. The emergency room visit happened in the middle of a dizzying night, pain so bad I wouldn't have cared what kind of shot they hit me with, lead or steel. They couldn't figure out why such a high white blood cell count, and I didn't know what to tell them other than just hit me with that shot, and quickly please. Awesome first responders, to treat a stranger as good as they treated me.

Off to a big hospital with more tests, one of them being this 2 hour long x-ray at a hulking claustrophobia machine called a HIDA scan. Finally and definitively they have isolated the source of the problem, the lining of the gallbladder, which means the whole thing must come out through a straw. I'm definitely cool with that, but they seemed reluctant and puzzled because no gall stones or other obvious causal connections. I told the very experienced capable doctor to please go after that red flaming pulsing organ on the CT scan, you know the unnecessary organ with all the red arrows pointing to it, and by the way, where do I sign. He did great, and in post op still wondered what I had done wrong to my body. I gave him my list of vices and added that I had been fighting with Lyme disease for seven years and marriage for 25. He blew all of that off saying; "no effect on gallbladder," "no effect on gallbladder," "this no make sense." It must have been the two therapeutic beers a day, because he said I should back off of alcohol, or next it will be my liver. I mused, tell that to Duke, 47 beers a day and he still has his liver, no car no more, no horse no more, no wife no more, but he's still got a liver, and a gallbladder!

Of course recovery hurt, but not near as bad as before surgery. I lost a little too much weight during that time and had to make myself eat to get back to the minimum 200 lbs., so I could still be in the pen with the herd bulls. I eventually did a deep dig into what in the heck just happened to me. Could the competent doctor be wrong and this all be attributable to Lyme disease? Finally, on some dead end internet feed I found a gal relating her experience with Lyme, infected gall bladder lining and all the same symptoms. Is this how the body works its miracle to expel such a pestilence, by sticking it into an organ that is not necessary to sustain life, how neat is that! You got it here first, from that day on, no more Lyme! Now, I bite ticks!

Ticks and mice. Now why was it God said we needed them? The field mice are terrible around here. I think the bobcats are all too busy at night doing things other than mousing as evidenced by the two new types of cats I speculate are in the area. I call one the RobertsHill cat, a cross between a Bobcat and a mountain lion, they have the underbelly markings of a bobcat fading into a solid black or solid fawn upper coat with a tail that isn't bobbed, but isn't long either. The other speculative type I noticed this spring was a cat running between my farm and the neighbor Amish farm that was generally the size of a big Tom cat, had a short tail and long back legs that just screamed "I've

---

got bobcat in me". My teenage son even muttered once that "it almost has rabbit-like back legs, and a short tail." Since that was the first time he talked to Dad during morning chores in eight years I thought this observation was significant. I explained to him that a rabbit, while it may be an active little fellow, probably did not get friendly with a barn cat. The chances were better that a bobcat got friendly with a barn cat. Then I asked him if he needed the talk about the birds and the bees. Luckily he declined saying, "I'm good dad." Anyway, the mystery cat had tiger stripes like a barn cat but all my sensibilities told me it was a crossbred. He or she (never got close enough to sex it because I didn't want my face ripped apart) even moved awkwardly until it would run, then it was faster than greased lightning. It spooked easily and after about two weeks, no more sightings, I'm figuring the call of the wild. This cross is harder to name, perhaps I'll go directly for a scientific name; Felinimous hybrid-bobtailimous. I'm working on verification of these crosses, but it's tough without DNA, ask any Bigfooter. The internet says this stuff does not happen and I'm fixing to be the first to prove the internet wrong. If this stuff doesn't happen then how did we get coy dogs out of coyotes, Ligers out of lions and tigers, Grolars out of grizzlies and polar bears, and every good crossed out mutt tough farm dog I've ever had?

I once lost a car in the shuffle of spring planting, finally I asked the kids if anyone knew where the Impala got off to. I would have blamed a local cowboy named Duke, but he was only stealing H-brand (Homeless brand) cattle at the time and not cars, especially since a horse is the last thing he had a license to drive. Two weeks went by and I'm running out of spotter vehicles so I pulled a "detective Monk," turns out the Impala was left by yours truly hidden on the back side of a hill in a hay meadow right where I had started planting. It ran a little rougher than normal coming home, so I checked the air filter and found it had been chewed through by a hungry field mouse and made into an odor bomb of a nest. Anything parked on grass around here is a mouse target! The moral to this story is, not even straight gravel dust breathed into the intake of an '03 Impala can kill that great car. If only I was that tough!

25.

Moron Mice

I spread some manure, not just in this book, but for other farms also. I was working on a local ranch hauling bale ring manure out onto the many beautiful but steep and rough acres of pasture. The pasture bounced me around so much that I developed these extra layers of stomach muscles, we call them "Coors muscles", they're hard to lose once you build them. In the cab of this tractor was a water bottle, well a repurposed plastic tea bottle with labels all over it, it sufficed in cool weather as a water jug. I'd take a swig every now and then and while bouncing around must have failed to screw the lid on enough and apparently my bouncy seat dislodged the lid and it probably sat overnight that way. Didn't even think twice about the lid being off as I was probably sliding sideways down some ski slope part of the pasture, on the ready to shut the pto off while jackknifing or as my son would call it "drifting". This run of manure spreading was probably three days long and on the last day the south wind was finally getting that first spring hot volatile weather thing going. Of course I was trying to beat a rain, always a race against the weather, and I was pushing it to get pasture and hay manure done, with planting right around the corner. The hot spring wind had me going through the rest of the water bottle fast. I debated on whether or not to call the kids to bring more, but instead decided to tough it out and ration what little was left. Finally toward evening I decided to kill the bottle, just enough water to get me across the finish line. When you don't have enough water, water is the only thing you can think about. My parched lips hit the bottle and started to gulp down those last precious ounces, but instead of a clear mountain stream taste I noticed a taste like old mushrooms. Not that I drink old mushrooms a lot. I didn't want to spit it out because every drop mattered, I was seriously thirsty. I thought maybe the bottle had dried up tea in the bottom when I loaded it, but a peek inside to the bottom divulged the culprit, a partially undressed field mouse swollen and starting to shed hair. Looked like he had been lifting weights or at least taking steroids. At the sight of this now beached once floating thing, I was very thankful the mouse itself had not gone down the hatch.

I wiped my lips off hoping no mouse hair was embedded in my cracked lips, my mouth tasted of varmint swill and I started to wonder how many days ago was it that the lid was off my water bottle. I tried to get the mouse tea back out of me but to no avail, surprised I couldn't elicit the desired reflex, not even with the help of an index finger that had pulled concrete chunks out of the manure pile. I had to think hard about hemorrhagic disease treatment strategies, but since I had failed to take any animal science classes at the big U, I decided to channel my inner Duke. I shall treat with whiskey.

Luckily my 16 year old dutiful daughter answered the phone call. I asked her to grab a glass, bring me some whiskey, and get a move on, please! She showed up to the field carrying a shot glass full of beautiful medicinal whiskey, this should help kill the germs. I put it down the hatch and told her to just leave me the whole bottle. "Uh Dad, I only brought you this shot glass full." Unbelievable. I made the mistake again of not being specific enough with the females in my life, but I knew I was in the wrong because I did not specifically say, "bring me the bottle of whiskey." As if there was ever any doubt, I am now sure my daughter is my wife's offspring, and was doing her level best to postpone my certain descent into the burning chasms of hell. I was more immediately concerned about the burning chasm of bacterial infections in my gut. She returned with the bottle within a half hour and I immediately took another swig. Not a big fan of whiskey, but I had to self medicate, so I watched my dosage and swear to God I only got about three fingers out of the fifth (about 2.5 inches) and the tractor got more and more powerful and taller, all the songs on the radio suddenly had a more profound meaning, and finally the tractor seemed to not care where it turned. I would've eaten a PB&J, to soak it up a bit, but those sandwiches usually don't even last till noon, and its almost dark. Moral to this part of the story, "don't drink whiskey on an empty stomach", unless you have to amputate part of your body with a pocket knife or kill mouse-borne diseases.

When I got to the house later that night I tried to act normal but the grin on my face was too permanent to pass off as normal. The kids had stupidly parked their bikes too close to the front door, I fell into them in a heap and was surprised how comfortable a bunch of bike pedals felt. Jill convinced me that I could not sleep there on the bikes, the shop part of the barn would be better.

That was about all I remember as the bacteria or something cost me my memory for the rest of the night. The next morning I did chores as normal, maybe a shade later and grayer. I was quite happy that I was not growing little buck teeth and whiskers. I got home from chores and told Jill I was so impressed that I felt as good as I did without worshiping the porcelain goddess or anything. She said, with a little bit of attitude, "David, what do you mean, we put a chair in front of the toilet and you were barfing for hours." The kids said, "yea Dad, if you were from Camelot they'd call you Sir Barfalot." Turnabout is fair play. Anyway, I used it as a teachable moment, telling the kids that I could have been taken advantage of that night, in my own house, by my own wife, and never even known it…a scenario which was highly probable judging from the circumstances.

I still can't think of a better way to get the desired results. You need to kill the germs, then remove the source of germs. I think I accomplished both. Now you know one potential treatment option for mouse tea. I still have trouble with the smell of whiskey to this day, but strangely enough I've developed this keen fondness for nibbling on cheese!

26.

Big Picture Rural Economic Health, Social Security and the Red Ford Ranger

I realize these rural policy problems I am trying to address are all first world problems, but if we don't change our selfish short sighted economic policies, our kids and grandkids will inherit a third world nation. Washington D.C. types always want to engineer themselves into relevance, but the majority of rural folks live a pretty conservative lifestyle, we really don't want government taxing and spending and providing for everyone. Can you give us a little space here! We don't need nearly as much federal government as we see and we really don't think taxpayers should be on the hook for an Obama phone, or for anyone's junk food, or especially college debts! Housing and health care and food, maybe help, but not a free ride. We want D.C. to leave us alone, protect our nation, protect our borders, protect our constitutional rights and make sure everyone is getting a fair chance at the American dream.

I think we still believe in a version of "responsible" capitalism built upon a Henry Ford principle where the worker at the plant should get paid enough to afford the product he or she is building. In other words the working class and for sure the business class can all participate in the economy and any person can become a part of the working class, then the business class. Short of the physically or mentally impaired, whom as a Christian society we have an obligation to help, we for sure do not need to help the rich get more subsidies. We do not need to help "campaign finance contributors" get more favorable policy. We do not need to pick winners and losers through the farm bill or any other bill. All "we" as the government need to do is make sure the game is being played fair.

Speaking of fair, I can't help but bring up our retirement system, Social Security. A system so many in the USA are banking on, including yours truly(not totally, but in part). It's such a political football where some say we must leave it just the way it is, it needs no fix. Folks with privileged jobs, matched 401Ks, or congressional retirement packages, say go ahead and make them work till they are 70. Others say it doesn't matter, it'll be broke by 2036 and it will go away, still others say 2036 will only mean a slight 20% reduction in benefits. I think most of us can agree that if we are going to have this kind of retirement system we better fund it....or else develop a pathway to replace it so future generations can make a plan. It's not good enough or fair to say to our kids, "it may or may not be there for you." Politicians on both sides who are not dealing seriously with this issue ought to be ashamed. I vote no on proposals asking me to be 70 years old for first access, that's not a serious plan.

So many things about Social Security(SS) have problems with fairness. First, all lower and middle class workers pay in at a rate of 6.2%, matched by their employers 6.2%, that's where the fairness stops. Self employed people (like farmers) have to pay both contributions, equalling 12.4%.... this makes self employment tax a tough one on us. You may consider this unfair, but listen to the rest of the story. High wage earners get a big break on SS tax. If your income goes above the payroll max at $168,800, then you are done paying in for the year. So, if you make double that income $338,000, you're down to paying only 3.1% of your annual income to SS tax, yet according to the social security administrations quick calculator, you still gain in benefits. Using the quick calculators default settings, a $168,800 income will get you $2528/mo. retirement benefit at age 63. Whereas at $338,000 you would get $2962/mo., a significant increase with no extra contribution. $500,000 income gets $2964 and 1 million dollar incomes get $2964. Wouldn't a continuation of the 6.2% tax until at least $338,000 be a good place to start refunding SS. I'll make the argument that if this country wants to continue to socialize retirement, all wage earners should continue to pay at 6.2%, the internet says that would secure it financially, and I'll bet they're right. Why should this system be carried on the backs of the lower and middle class worker and the self-employed of any class.

Another unfair situation from the social security taxation standpoint is the exemption from paying it on income earned from passive investment in land and rental properties, advantaging landlords over renters. Right now I try to farm most of my land and derive an income from actively farming it, any precious profit is subject to a 12.4% tax from social security. Yet, if I quit farming and rented it all out, I would not have to pay social security tax on any of the income derived from renting it out, only back to the tax on additional income which contributes to your nominal tax rate. Not very fair to Social Security is it? Who do you think designed that system, and why do you think we have so many absentee landlords renting out farmland? Tax policy makes a big impact on business behavior. Shouldn't the landlords (renters) at least share in the S.S. tax burden with the guy farming it, 6.2/6.2 each. To make matters worse for S.S., now consider the fact that farmers sometimes lose money even when all the rent gets paid to the landlord. What this means is that there are years where the social security administration gets no money at all from the farmer or the landlord. Wouldn't it make sense to guarantee 6.2% every year, year after year after year by Social Security taxing rental income.

I say, fund social security or start phasing it out with a real plan. Shouldn't the farm lobby be "all in" for social security tax burdens to shift to a 6.2/6.2 split between farmer and landlord. It might be hard to get Congressmen and Land Grant Economists who are landowners to agree, but what do you say we get them on record.

Final thoughts on big picture socialized security. The system was designed by FDR in 1935 for the "greatest generation" who did a whole lot for this country but have never been afraid of borrowing on generations to come. Then the "baby boomers" came along selfishly spending on social programs because they were supposed to have it easier than their folks, they never saw debt they didn't mind passing along to their kids. All you hear from those two generations is how the next generation and the one after that, and the one after that, doesn't want to work anymore. Not only do these up and coming generations have to work, now they have to clean up for the selfishly designed system which after only two generations is destined to go broke. Gen X/millennials/gen Z will have to clean up the mess, or else drown in it.

On, from the not so poor to the rural poor. It's important for us to not project our own version of a comfortable existence onto the lower income folks in rural USA, the D.C. version of success may be measured in dollars, theirs measured in time. You'd be surprised how cheap some of these industrious people can live. No state or federally subsidized college education for many of them, just regular old non-privileged jobs to make ends meet. A lot of them choose less income over "the hamster wheel". Many of them get a pay raise when they retire, when social security checks start coming in. The Amazon van may not even know how to get to their county. Possessions are not their preoccupation. They live by the old adages, "you never see a Hurst with a luggage rack", or "a funeral procession with a Brinks truck."

I had an interesting experience with this "time" thing in rural almost West Virginia, Ohio, where I was desperately trying to get to a meeting with my crop insurance boss, seems my red ford ranger's transmission breather tube got plugged with mud from my creek crossing and eventually started overheating my tranny every 30 miles or so. Since I couldn't figure out the source of my problem quick enough, I would rest the truck when it happened. I ended up sitting on three porches that Saturday (hey, maybe that's where "sat"urday got its name), two in small Appalachian communities and one at my boss's folks' porch.

Never was I denied a friendly visit and when I told them of my peril most could "one-up" me. One of my favorite stories was from the guy who told tale of meeting a proud rancher who was bragging up the size of his ranch and how the neat old 1948 ranch pickup they had as a kid was displayed proudly out front the ranch to this day, said "they could drive that '48 all day and not get from one end of the ranch to the other," to which the Appalachian fellow said, "yeah, when our '48 Ford got that bad last year, we just took it to the junkyard." There was something about that day's experience told me to slow down and enjoy the ride. Their wealth was in the time they could spend with family, or to visit with a stranger, or to watch it rain. The rural culture had just showed its good side, but now for the rest of the story. Anyone else miss Paul Harvey?

It may be appropriate at this point to channel my inner Indian chief and make a distinction between the "broken spirit" vs. the "lower income" folks of rural USA. Some lower income may even identify themselves as Hillbilly, but that does not mean they are broken in spirit. We all have a little Hillbilly in us, and as a friend once said, "The nice thing about Hillbillies, you know right where you stand with them real quick, because they don't have a phony filter." Self-identified hillbillies are direct with you, rarely in need of government assistance because of their independent nature, they don't want government's help and they definitely don't want to be told how to live their lives. In the part of rural Ohio where I was raised and farmed, many people were removed from the hill part of hillbilly by only one generation. I always loved how they would fondly relate stories of their past or how a visit down to the hollers in Kentucky or West Virginia would remind them what little they had as kids. Some would say that's why they left, others would say they should've never left. The reality is that jobs were especially hard to find once the coal mining left, then tobacco mostly left. So the way into jobs was to the north on U.S. highway 23, right into central Ohio. The colloquial reference to that move northward was the "three Rs," Reading/Righting/Rt.23 illustrating that yes it does happen in every state that the state to the north always has to "throw shade", metaphorically speaking, on its southern neighbor.

The local Amish kids think I studied a different version of the "three Rs" in school as a child, Reading/Riting/&Rithmetic. They see right through me and my joking around, even catching on to the one where I tell them I thought I saw where their new baby foal (horse) might be sick because I noticed he was a "little horse". If the Amish lifestyle is judged by the brightness of their kids, they're doing something right for sure. Talk about kids who are raised with very little in the realm of possessions.

The starter farm I bought in Central Ohio had this character of an old man as father to the neighbor. That old man could tell such great stories; he and 11 siblings had come out of that hill country. He even got a wife out of there, said he found her on Fifth and Plum (I'm thinking that's a notably tough downtown Cincinnati street crossing, she didn't strike me as a *working woman*, if you know what I mean.) "Yeah," he says, "fifth ridge back and plum up against the hill!" What a neat thing to hear those stories of old Appalachia, how my neighbor's granddad would butcher a hog and smoke his own bacon and eat it with his grits and eggs every morning into his 90s, skinny as a bean pole, sharp as a tack, busy as a beaver, until old granddad turned the tasty varmint into a pair of water proof waders.

Now for the broken spirit side of rural America. The rest of the story ties back to the Red Ford Ranger truck again. The tranny was fatally damaged that day by the heat buildup, but did get me home. The truck didn't owe me a thing, got parked for a while since the only thing it could be traded for was probably worse. This young kid who did some salvage metal scraping in the area stopped by at Christmas time to see if our farm needed any vehicles or farm equipment scrapped out or worked on, he could use some money/work before Christmas bills come due and all. I had worked with him once before, so I went with Jesus here and gave preferential treatment to the poor, gave him $300 cash for a junkyard transmission and told him he would get the rest of the money when the Red Ford Ranger was back up and running. Down the road he went with the truck on his trailer.

Months went by, then phone calls went unanswered. I eventually found where they lived and saw the truck in the backyard, with a large tree stump in it. I knocked on the door and was surprisingly invited into the house where people laid around on couches like they had just participated in a meth orgy. The T.V. was stuck on the "Price is Right", which is totally ironic. I had my first official encounter with white trash right there in their own trash den. I stood there amazed at how pathetic and depressing the whole scene was. For a while I couldn't see them very well so I cracked the door open in preparation for a quick escape and to shed a little light in the dark room, as it was the middle of the day, sunny and bright outside. The light illuminated cloths and food containers everywhere. Dentures on an end table. My conscience had a battle between sympathy, empathy and anger, but never envy. For the first time in my life I felt really tall, that's because everyone else was laying down and did not get up. They lied to me about how they were working on the truck and I laid the gauntlet down that I would haul it away in two weeks if it wasn't done.

Two weeks came, no call of course, dah! I went to get the truck and imagine that, it was gone. No vehicles at all. Am I in the right yard, yes, there is the stump that was in the bed. The people were gone, the mess was there, but no Red Ford Ranger. Across the way I spy a convenience store, WIC, Cigs and Lottery tickets, all the necessities. The owner informed me that the trashy people had gotten kicked out of the rental house. He said they got the Red Ford Ranger running, then used it to move out of town. When I asked where they moved, he wasn't sure. I've had some tough moves also, but never in a stolen truck! I called the town cops to see if they knew where the thieving varmints went, he said, "Hopefully far away, those people are not allowed inside corporation limits again."

Again, I can rationalize almost anything and I figured I had done the whole town a favor by giving them a ride outta Dodge. The thank you letter from the town cops never came. I reported the truck stolen, canceled the liability insurance and lamented its loss to a very unsympathetic wife. The tongue lashing went something like this, "You should've known that was going to happen. How much did you pay them to steal your truck, d.a.?" D.A. is not short for district attorney in this case.

Oh wait, there's more. The funny thing was, I got a call a

month or two later from the boss who I was late getting to. He said a Red Ford Ranger with a fitting description was fished out of a lake down his way. Seems like the thieves were heading toward God's country, West Virginia. My boss had the gall to find the whole incident somewhat amusing, but he'd seen it all from his days of growing big acres of tobacco in the heart of tobacco country Appalachia; he has way more of these kinds of stories than I do.

The moral to this Red Ford Ranger story is that all the help in the world, all the food stamps in the USDA, and all the generosity of a church or food pantry wasn't going to help this group of broken spirits get their lives together. Unfortunately, as we all well know, the more money some of these types get, the more drugs/alcohol and addictive behavior they get, and even worse, it becomes a generational thing. I don't pretend to know the answer to this complex problem, but I do know throwing taxpayer money at the problem is obviously not working. I am guessing jobs and individual opportunity to participate in the American dream are the solution and key to rural economic health and hope, we need some serious policy reform. No doubt this family of lost souls would be better off scratching around in their own garden in near total poverty, than moving from town to town, rental to rental, and government handout to government handout.

Some rural jobs do not pay very good wages and obviously welfare programs can sometimes pay better than working, especially when children are involved. So let's consider taking a different look at minimum wage to accommodate businesses who need cheap inexperienced labor and families who need to make more jingle. Below is my not-so-famous "Wedding Cake Graph" for indexing minimum wage for age. Not famous because when I propose this to presidential candidates as they come through the High School commons at Caucus time they look back up at me with their eyes crossed and then do a "work around" to shake someone's hand who was not at all previously engaged. The idea for different minimum wages is to give that kid in high school a chance to start somewhere and lose the phone a minute or two while he/she gets some real work done for a real boss, but at the lowest tier of minimum wage

@ $9/hr. Then when one graduates high school and gets a little more serious about contributing to society (ages 18-26), he/she should have gained the skills to get to the next tier @ $13/hr. The top tier wages (ages 26-62) @ $17/hr. goes to the age group of "no more parental insurance" up to social security retirement because this is the age group with families and more real financial burdens. Then at retirement age (62+), since you can't earn as much anyway, but now can receive SS benefits we go back down to the high school kids wage level so that you can work side by side to teach them what life was like before cell phones and they can teach you how the use the self checkout line. Remember, a minimum wage stops no one from getting an employer to recognize their value with more pay. From my perch it sure looks like a bit more wage for the lower income in rural America could help.

"Proposed Minimum Wage Graphic"
-Opinion of Author

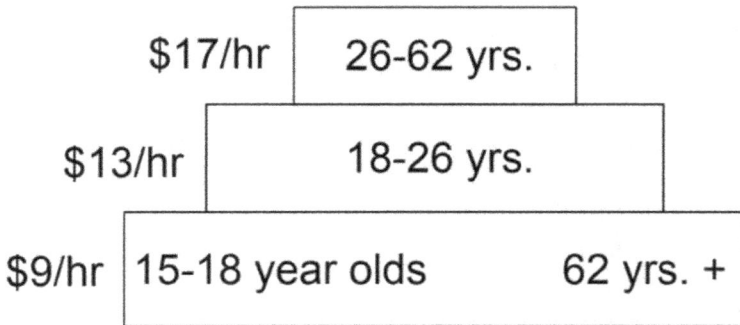

$17/hr	26-62 yrs.	
$13/hr	18-26 yrs.	
$9/hr	15-18 year olds	62 yrs. +

Rural America has been injured by bad government policy coming from multiple directions. From welfare dependency to tax policy to farm programs that create haves and have-nots.

A definition of the American dream is impossible to pin down, it changes for every individual and that's exactly as our founders and our creator would want it, I hope. I can only speak for myself. My American dream revolves around *freedom* and *ownership* of sufficient land (the amount of which is self-determined,) using the business of farming as a way to accomplish both while raising a family. So much opportunity for rural people to own land has been taken away by government ownership of western lands and by tax policies and subsidies that concentrate land into fewer and fewer hands. Not only do all the aforementioned USDA programs contribute to this acquisition and bigness phenomenon, estate tax law and capital gains tax law and 1031 "like-kind" tax deferred exchanges also influence the financial landscape of rural America, making farmland almost unattainable to those who are not playing the USDA farm game in a big way, or fortunate enough to have multigenerational wealth, or development property.

I am not an expert on estate tax law, but since we desire to leave something of value for the next generation we do pay attention. Land being the largest asset for most farmers has inflated substantially over my lifetime. It is important from a fairness perspective that an estate can reestablish the basis (price you paid to purchase + improvements) for land value at the time of an estate owner's death, this is called a "step up in basis" and it reflects "fair market value", so that subsequent sales of that ground will not be subject to the previous owner's gain, whether it be inflation induced or not. In 2023 an estate will have no "death tax" from the feds if it's worth less than $12.9 million, some states have decoupled from the feds to get more taxes. Let's say unmarried Farmer B has an estate worth $13.9 million and he does the same thing every one of us is going to do.... he up and dies, and can't take it with him. The people inheriting the estate will get an estate tax bill of 40%(death tax) on the $1 million overage, that is a ridiculously huge number, and hence may require land to be sold off just to pay tax, in this example; $400,000 in tax. Now, if Farmer B was married, the couple could build the estate tax monies to an effective combined "death tax" exclusion of $25.8 million in 2023. If you're worth anywhere near that kind of money please consult an estate tax advisor and don't reference this book to the feds, they'll just laugh.

The exercise above shows how much wealth can be protected and concentrated in families and therefore when properly planned, land does not have to sell off. Corporate structuring begins to play a role at these higher estate values also, tying up land and assets in the corporation. While the tax rate of 40% is for sure too high, maybe the exclusion rate is also too high at $12.9 million a person, creating a shortage of land on the market, also creating some pretty wealthy families. Big Ag organizations like the Farm Bureau lobby for large exclusions for the death tax. Instead, they should be lobbying for my next proposal, **"indexing capital gains for duration of ownership."**

The current capital gains tax arrangement also keeps land off the market and has always bothered me. It is unfair to older farmers and effectively discourages them from selling land because it taxes them on inflation. Let's say Farmer C has a piece of land he purchased in 1970 for $1,000/A and sells in 2023 for $10,000/A. To the government that is a $9000/A capital gain (minus some basis improvements perhaps)....or is it? I believe capital gains should be "indexed for duration of ownership." Let's look at what inflation did to that land value during the 53 years he owned it. The land inflated to $7914, according to the calculator on the web using the U.S. Bureau of Labor Statistics CPI inflation worksheet. I'm thinking someone will say CPI is the wrong way to figure land inflation and I would be willing to listen. Back to the big picture, in other words $1000 in 1970 had the same buying power $7914 has today using all the assumptions in the CPI calculator. I maintain that when Farmer C sells in 2023 he should only have to pay capital gains tax on $10,000 minus $7914 = $2086, multiplied by a capital gains rate of 15% = $313/A instead of the at least $1350/A the feds currently want. States will also get their pound of flesh but at lower rates, unless Farmer C is lucky enough to live in a state that waves it.

Most of us are okay with a responsible amount of taxation, but you can see how this unfair capital gains policy provides a disincentive for a farmer to sell land vs. keeping it in the estate and getting a "step up" in basis for the heirs of the estate. I think we could increase the amount of land that comes on the market if we could at least "index for duration of ownership" on all farmland capital gains, it may help with the transition of land to the next generation while providing opportunities for more people to own farmland... or to at least scratch around in their own garden.

The last bad tax policy for rural America is the 1031 like-kind exchange which is a way to *defer* paying capital gains tax by rolling capital gains into the next property purchased. Eventually those taxes have to be paid. Many rules have to be followed to qualify, and time is ticking on these exchanges. Sometimes you will see a piece of land go for way above market price and you can only figure someone's clock was about to expire on a 1031. But yes! apartment buildings and industrial properties can be used to buy farmland in this exchange, it's not just farmland to farmland. I say *Index capital gains* taxes for duration of ownership and you no longer need to offer the 1031 exchange.

Government policies that concentrate ownership of assets into the hands of fewer people: bad for rural America. Government policies that encourage more individuals to own assets: good for rural America. Earned ownership is the ultimate route to responsible behavior and prideful people. Tax policies and USDA involvement have taken us in the wrong direction, that's why I say a lot of rural America's problems are top down, just regular old bad policy. We're going to need some legislative help here.

27.

Corn and the Food vs. Fuel Debate

Corn. The Indians called it maize. They developed it out of the teosinte plant 9000 years ago in southern Mexico. It became a very important source of food as it is the main ingredient for tortillas, a staple food in the Mexican diet. The corn tortilla is the most important food in Mexico to this day. Interestingly and ironically Mexico went from inventing corn and the use of corn for food, originally using native varieties, switching to hybrid corn and fertilizers during Norman Borlaug's "green revolution" of the mid 20th century, to subsidized commercialized farming of corn in the 70s and 80s, to NAFTA agreements to buy from the U.S. in the 90s and 2000s, and finally to a tortilla crisis by 2007, with the price of the staple food rising way ahead of the rate of inflation. It seems like it's been an unfortunate steady downhill slide for the corn tortilla in Mexico and it looks like it is even an important political football for the country. They appear to be even ahead of us in losing their small and mid-sized farms, perhaps that is why so many of their youth are heading north.

Now, here in 2023/2024 there is still a tortilla issue in Mexico and the U.S. is involved. In an article from Reuters dated June 19, '23 they report, "[Mexico's] President Obrador to sign an agreement this week with makers of the country's food staple tortilla that ensures they only use non-genetically modified white corn while also setting new tariffs on imports of the grain. Tariffs on white corn imports with countries that do not have trade deals with Mexico will promote more domestic purchases." Further it is reported by Reuters that "[the U.S. has] trade disputes over Obradors decree to limit the use of GM (genetically modified) corn, particularly for human consumption, since nearly all imports come from U.S. suppliers."

Basically, Mexico wants non-GMO corn at least for its tortillas, and the U.S. wants them to take GMO corn to satisfy our trade deals and our commodity associations. Since no one has called me to settle this trade problem, my opinion here probably does not matter. But I'm going to give it anyway because I have had some interesting experiences in this arena, and since experience is an expensive but effective teacher, here we go.

President Obrador is right, not just because "the customer is always right" as I learned in my training with the big chemical company, but because the rats say so. The mice say so. The coons say so. The deer say so. The cows and the pigs say so sometimes. So why don't we just grow the corn Mexico wants for food, identity preserve it, get a premium and get on with the job of exporting a desired product? It's no trick to grow non-GMO (genetically modified organism) corn unless your fields are surrounded by woods, because the deer and coons will eat the heck out of non-GMO corn.

Please don't confuse non-GMO corn with organic corn like the young fella from the corn growers group might have. I went to a corn growers association meeting last summer encouraging them to be more customer focused and willing to promote non-GMOs in order to get into so many of these export markets that we have lost. A young confident kid whom I presented this idea to, you would have thought I asked him to grow corn with no herbicides, insecticides, fungicides, fertilizers or free seed corn hats, kind of like organic corn does. I'm not sure he knew that non-GMO corn is still being grown by some farmers voluntarily, especially in the fringes of the corn belt where European Corn borer populations are lower and less injurious to yield. The cost of a non-GMO seed bag may be around $180/

bag when the same hybrid in a GMO seed is $300/bag. A buddy of mine had a bunch of very high yielding corn in '24 in Ohio and didn't see a difference in his non-GMO corn yield vs. GMO corn yield. He didn't even grow it to enroll in a special identity preserved program with a premium, like we both used to do. The problem has slowly become that seed corn suppliers do less and less development of hybrids getting $180/bag than hybrids getting $300/bag. So as a result GMO corn hybrids are continually taking over. Gmos in corn once had the advantage of being easier to manage, but now they have been around long enough that insect and weed resistance has made it necessary to go back to many of the chemical inputs we used before GMOs arrived as an option. No chemical inputs are allowed in the organic corn production arena and yields are usually significantly lower but financial compensation per bushel can make it worthwhile. Weeds and lots of tillage, and especially sandal wearing certifiers are my negative experiences with organic production. Loved the premiums!

Back in the 2006-2008 timeframe I was growing non-GMO corn to sell at a Cincinnati grain terminal on the Ohio River. I received a reasonable premium paid, about 35 cents per bushel plus I could pick up considerable basis improvement (basis = the difference between Chicago board of trade price and local market price, also called "legalized theft" by some other cynics) by hauling it 90 miles to the river. The process was very simple, they would sample the load and you would pull to the side for 15-20 minutes while they ran a lab test to determine the purity of your load. I was never rejected for GMO contamination from cross pollination, but knew this could be an issue. The only load I ever had rejected, had an off odor that came from the equivalent of a bushel basket full of moldy kernels around one of those little crawl through doors on an old Silver Shield bin. Lesson learned, it does not take much spoiled grain to ruin a whole 900 bushel truckload.

92% of corn and 94% of beans in the U.S. are GMOs. On my farm I went from 100% non-GMO 8 years ago to 100% GMOs from then until today. The deer and coon were eating me alive on these non-GMO fields surrounded by pasture and woods. I got tired of being the neighborhood trap crop for furry things. Now I look for hybrids the critters from the woods do not like. Call it survival of the fittest for farmer Dave. I found a winning white cob GMO hybrid with about every genetic modification modern science can offer. It will keep its ear from being eaten by anything way up past harvest, even on the outside rows! If you leave the shelled corn from that hybrid in front of them long enough the cows will eventually eat it, but I'm not saying they prefer it. The corn stalk round bales of this hybrid make better bedding than feed for the cows, they'd rather lie in it than eat on it. Occasionally I find a GMO hybrid or soybean variety that the critters do like, but generally my overall plan has worked. Sometimes I even include a bottle of cheap aftershave in the spray tank around the outside rows, maybe that's why the bobcats are always cat'n around at night.

Back in the late 90s when GMO seeds were first emerging, farmers were dipping their toes in the water, testing these new expensive seeds for relative value. As they started getting some use, we heard colloquial rumors of lower conception rates in gestating pigs, squirrels that wouldn't eat cobs at the squirrel feeder and people planting them specifically around wooded draws to ward off the furry things, much like I do today. At first I wasn't "all-in" on these GMO/non-GMO differences, but I sure respected the people I heard the stories from. The next experience was all my own and it shocked me.

Rats: I'm not a big fan of them but they sure liked my pig barn. My seed corn was stored in a barn next to the pig barn and the darned cats had this deal with the rats where they would maintain a steady population of breeder rats who in turn supplied a steady stream of naive babies. Of course this was a good deal for the cats as the youngsters were much easier for the lazy cats to catch, and tender too. It was about 2003, I was testing a GMO hybrid against its non-GMO sister hybrid in my little test plot, so I had a partial sampler bag of GMO corn left over. I held onto it for a while to make sure I wouldn't need it for replant seed. A month or two after planting, while attempting a general farm cleanup, I saw the bag was eaten on and it smelled like a rodent party. As I was heading for the garbage I peeked into the bag to find a rats nest of ripped up plastic and brown bag liner, thankfully no rat, but the bag still had weight to it like it wasn't all chaff. With my gloved hand I reached down into the bag, and pulled out something really scary. Untouched, un-nibbled upon, germs not eaten, kernels complete, perfect looking seed corn. Normally every germ would be eaten and all you'd have left was a bag of smelly chaff. Nope, not a single kernel eaten. Needless to say, all those stories from two or three years ago started replaying in my mind, could this all be true, never in my life of dealing with farm stuff would you have ever seen this. It's like seeing the coyote lying down with the lamb, well at least a live lamb that's not in said coyote's mouth.

Maybe we could chalk that one up to the seed treatment, maybe that was it, the seed corn supplier agreed, that was probably what we were seeing. Until the mice told us differently. The next year a very good seed salesman successfully talked me into splitting my planter for a test plot of non-GMO vs GMO, half and half in a twelve row planter, I could get a really good deal cause I was a new customer. He didn't say, "but look out next year when you're an old customer, you'll get a 20% price increase and won't even get a seed corn hat. So I took six bags of each and stacked them on a pallet, side by side, same seed treatment, should be a good comparison of technology perfor-mance. Instead, it was a good comparison of mouse preference. The freaking mice got right up the middle and as I pulled bags away the non-GMO bags were leaking onto the GMO bags. Not a single GMO bag was broken into, unbelievable, they must smell the difference all the way through the seed bag, how can that be? The salesman missed one of the best selling points, he should've said, "nothing will touch your seed prior to planting this GMO hybrid, if the goats get out, the pigs get out, the cows get out, the rats get out, you're good to go!"

Lest you think I am the only backwards farmer that would have ever seen this seed phenomenon, guess again. A seed dealing buddy of mine with a real seed warehouse called me out of the blue one year after witnessing the same seed/mice/non-GMO vs. GMO phenomenon, said he had gone 6 or seven years thinking I was a wack job, but now had some doubt about doubting his old buddy. His experience was on a big bulk bag of non-GMO corn sitting next to the same hybrid in the GMO version, both with the same seed treatment. Once again, mice ate through the even heavier canvas of these bulk bags to feast on the non-GMO corn seed. We both agreed it was troubling but didn't know what to do with that.

Just this winter of '24 an Amish man was telling me his pig story. The Amish grow pigs the old fashioned way, spoiled, right up to the day they go from pig to pork! The fellow had planted open pollinated seed so that he could save the seed and plant the kernels next year without having to purchase new expensive seed, also avoiding all the hassle the seed corn industry does to create a hybrid. That open pollinated corn was going to cost him less than $2/A in seed cost, it's right out of the wagon and into the planter. You betcha I got me some of that. A hybrid yields at least double the yield of open pollinated, but takes a lot more to produce. Seed corn companies have to grow two different inbred lines close in proximity to one another and hire busloads of high school kids and a lot of "porta johns" to detassel the female line, then destroy the ears of the male line(unless using a male sterile inbred). Hybrid vigor is neat and results from crossing two inbred lines, you have to do a lot of selfing to get these.

Big picture, you can not get a thrifty plant out of the seed that goes into the grain bin from a hybrid, but you can out of an open pollinated corn. Anyway, the Amish pigs were being fed exclusively ears of this open pollinated corn until one day when a well meaning crop insurance adjuster stopped by (no three legged chickens in this story, I swear). He had probably been out doing hail claims from the derecho storm, assessing deferred ear damage which happened in the pre-tassel corn, the good hail insurance companies will let farmers defer the assessment in order to do a thorough job of assessing hail damage to ears that were in the bud pre-tassel. He threw his assessed ears out of the truck so the Amish fellow could feed these to the pigs, employing the old adage, "waste not, want not". Problem was, the pigs wouldn't eat these ears, and since this area is probably 100% GMO hybrids, with no vomitoxin problems, there's a pretty good chance those ears were all GMO, and the pigs didn't like that. Another example of an animal rejecting this stuff. I'm not saying the pig would never eat that corn, but it's not going to be first on the menu like the non-GMO corn, or the open pollinated corn.

We see this in our cattle where they won't go crazy for GMO corn, but if that's all they get, they'll eat it. Hybrids do make a difference and any hybrid GMO or non-GMO when afflicted with aflatoxin, resulting from aspergillus fungi, will also cause critters to turn up their nose. Also, any degree of processing seems to make animals like GMO corn more, from extruding to grinding, to pelletizing into corn gluten pellets, or byproducts like distillers grains, etc.

After all these experiences with critters and GMO hybrids, I have to say, maybe the President of Mexico and the Mexican people are onto something here. I try to respect what nature tells me and maybe nature is smarter than people, or at least maybe people are supposed to learn from what nature tells them. I don't want to put a GMO sweet corn hybrid in my garden, to eat directly off the cob when I am doing just fine with my non-GMO hybrid, not after all my real life experiences. Maybe corn should be more identity preserved and channeled per use. Right now, corn processed for people food is generally not separated or differentiated from corn going to an ethanol plant or a feed plant. With a few exceptions, there are not special hybrids for each use, we commingle everything for every commingled use resulting in a generic product to export that is probably 95+% GMO. A non-identity preserved crop makes it easier for shippers and elevators and farmers, resulting in the cheapest product we can offer.

Problem becomes, we can't export corn worth a darn anymore. For the last 20 years, USA corn exports are flat while Brazilian corn exports are up 11 fold. Apparently their Safrinha corn crop is the cheapest thing ever. Our current U.S. corn prices are 25% below the cost of production, $3.89/bu at our local elevator March 4, '24. All these years of paying a checkoff dollar to our big corn lobbyists and farmers are going backwards on price and on ability to produce a globally competitive product.

Meanwhile production continues to increase. It's a top down problem. Every time I hear a market analyst say, "export sales lagging," you have to wonder why they don't add, "Maybe we ought to take our buyers needs seriously and offer them what they want. Maybe we ought to be the value added suppliers in the world market." This is one of those conversations we are not allowed to have on farm radio, or as an industry, and if you tried, the attitude you would get back is that you were against progress. I ask, "how much progress is there in pathetic export numbers."

As of 2024, 64 countries around the world require GM foods to be labeled as such, including all E.U. countries, Australia, and Japan. That in itself does not eliminate the use of GMOs but it cuts real deep. 26 countries ban GMOs entirely. None of these countries mentioned include our number one trading partner in Mexico, whose ban is for corn used to produce tortillas only. I'm not even sure where we stand with China, they sometimes use new USA GMO technology to block our corn exports when it is convenient for them. There are currently no bans on GMO crops used for the USA market, we're all in, as am I because of my hairy critters of the woods problem. What premium would it take for me to go back to non-GMO production (me probably $1.00/bu., some maybe half that)? What premium would the world market pay for non-GMO production?? The latter is a question our industry needs to address because after 20+ years this problem for the U.S. corn industry is not going away.

Obviously, the GMO crops are not hurting our sow herd as farrowings have recently hit an all time high (good job pig guys). I think GMOs are not hurting our cattle feeding rate of gains as I have not heard any rumbling of problems there. Obviously, they are not hurting our yields as we just got done producing a record corn crop of 15.3 billion bu. Also, they are not hurting our agribusinesses because $300/bag seed corn and lots of high yield inputs work well for them. At one point I would have said GMOs reduce chemical inputs but nature keeps sending us resistant weeds and insects to do a work-around, so unfortunately that advantage went away. I'm down to two advantages for my farm, one being, repel the hairy woods critters and two being more convenience and options for herbicides. The herbicide convenience advantage is much greater in soybeans, not such a big deal in corn, therefore making non-GMO corn production easier than non-GMO soybean production.

Discussions of the food safety side of GMOs has been relegated to late night AM radio shows like Coast-to-Coast, where you are allowed to talk about anything, as long as it isn't vulgar, host George Noory does a good job of rejecting vulgarity. Since we heat our house with wood, my body is programmed to do the middle of the night stoking and sometimes I'll catch AM 1040 WHO radio (a 50,000 watt clear channel station)out of Des Moines on the topic of gut ailments/human health concerns associated with GMO foods. This topic obviously piques my interest because after 20+ years of being a professional crop observer, I'm wondering what objective science has learned. I think the human health and safety side of GMO's was left to a long term study of you/me/we as lab rats. Maybe because they couldn't get the real lab rats to eat it.

Almost every time I've heard the "GMOs in our food topic" on the radio there was at least a mention of "leaky gut syndrome" in humans. A condition where toxins and bacteria leak through the intestine wall and into the bloodstream. Symptoms include diarrhea, bloating and fatigue, oh and moodiness, which one would think comes hand and hand with diarrhea.

This leaky gut topic reminds me of the story farmers would hear all the time when we were first being sold this new technology in corn. The first Genetic modification to corn was the insertion of the Bt (Bacillus thuringiensis) microorganism, in 1996, which in turn prompted the plant to make a protein that caused a specific wormy insect class called lepidoptera to get a gut rupture and leak out, causing desiccation (dry out) and then death. First, they have to take that lethal bite of plant tissue. Really neat stuff. The Bt corn got rid of a lot of European corn borers, but was weak on cutworm, which is a real problem for no-tillers, also it had no efficacy on corn rootworm which is a monster pest in corn-on-corn rotations.

Obviously the first iteration of Bt had some holes in performance, so new versions to kill more insect pests are constantly being developed. One attempt, approved in 1998 caused a lot of problems for the US corn export market and ended up getting food products recalled. The Federation of American Scientists (2011) did an article on "The case study of Starlink™ corn" in which they said, "it contained a gene for a Bt toxin CRY9c. This toxin was heat resistant and did not break down readily in the human gastrointestinal tract suggesting it might be allergenic." As a result of this phenomenon the EPA restricted its use to animal feed use only. Problem was, the corn did some cross pollination, got commingled with every other type of corn and of course got in our food supply. In year 2000, we found it in foods, especially tacos, and massive food recalls ensued, soon after that, the corn product line was dropped. A large fast food chain dealt with a customer who claimed her anaphylactic shock health event was caused by tacos with the CRY9c event detected in them. The threat to human health as a gut irritant was real enough to end this particular Bt protein modification, but many other Bt modifications have been developed and inserted into our corn since then and even stacked one upon the other, but these other variants have passed the FDA tests.

Another example of a corn industry miscalculation with GMOs was the Viptera™ gene in corn, a trait which offered improved cutworm and earworm protection, not in human ears but on corn ears. I remember the attitude of our industry leaders to be, "go ahead and plant it, they will approve it by harvest" which turned out to be a bit arrogant and presumptive. In November of 2013 it was finally banned by China, two years after the seed containing the Viptera™ trait was marketed. This cost farmers enough export market, at least temporarily that lawyers got involved and class action lawsuits paid us pennies on the dollar for our losses, keeping farmers driving old Chevettes, while the lawyers all got new Corvettes. I remember multiple cargo vessels heading to Chinese ports had to be turned around and sold elsewhere for a discount. You can't tell me GMOs have not negatively affected our exporting abilities, that would be like taking a leak on my boots and telling me, "hey Dave, it's raining!"

Do you really think these smart scientists who work for the

FDA can rule out the possibility that something subacute is going on here to irritate the human gut? How can they even predict what synergism or antagonism happens in multiple food supplies with different stacked GMO events. It seems pretty obvious they have missed something here. Farmers have always been assured GMOs have no negative effects on beneficial insects, beneficial animals, or beneficial humans and we sure hope they are not contributing to the decline in beneficial bee populations. But really, how did the inventors know any of this without a 20 year study? Wait a minute, was I in that study?

Well, since we were all in that study without compensation, here is my own crackpot conclusion. Yes, our human guts are somewhat negatively affected by the presence of something in GMO plants and/or grains, probably a protein, some guts more sensitive than others. My gut for instance has been irritated by hemorrhagic disease, lyme disease and medicinal whiskey and therefore all the villi, defined as micro hairlike filaments on the gut wall, are probably burnt off. A fully functional healthy gut, however, may be more prone to irritation of the villi giving way to "celiac disease": a disease in which the small intestine is hypersensitive to gluten, leading to irritation and problems digesting foods. All the same symptoms of leaky gut disease, but I think there are even more complications. Celiac is classified as an autoimmune disorder. I feel bad for those who are afflicted, because the disease can cause constant discomfort. Fortunately, many gluten free food options now exist, but some have been criticized by the internet of still having corn glutens in them. The opinions are everywhere on celiac disease, from "it's no different than a belly-ache of 100 years ago" to, it's so debilitating that it can lead to Type 1 diabetes, Epilepsy, multiple sclerosis (MS), infertility and miscarriage, amongst other complications. I'm not sure, and am left still wondering, "what do the critters know that humans don't."

Gluten is a substance found in cereal grains, mainly wheat, responsible for the elastic texture of dough, it is the primary suspect in the celiacs problem. So celiac disease results from an irritation of the gut caused by the two proteins of wheat glutens interacting with what? Are GMO corn or soybean food products and their associated proteins setting the gut up to be irritated when a wheat gluten comes sliding through? Would the irritation still happen with non-GMO corn? Is the irritation an allergic reaction? Seems like the disease hardly existed prior to year 2000, when GMO corn started to get mainstreamed, see the following graphs. My gut feeling, pun intended, is that it's an irritation on top of an irritation. Kind of like when you go to pay your real estate taxes and find out landowners with USDA CRP contracts are getting a tax break, from the State!

How else am I to conclude after 20+ years of GMO experiences and a misappropriated honorary doctorate given to me from the USDA vet. Check out the degree of coincidence in the following graphs. Look at 2005 as the year GMO corn saturated 50% of corn grown in the U.S., then look at the second graph as we ate that corn in 2006. The onset of celiac disease fits pretty close to the onset of wide scale adoption of GMOs in the U.S., especially close to the blue line of corn. I know correlation does not mean causation, but someone ought to check this coincidence out, with real science and real fast. Even if you were a scientist working for the USDA or FDA, preoccupied with pronouns, this phenomenon should pique your interest.

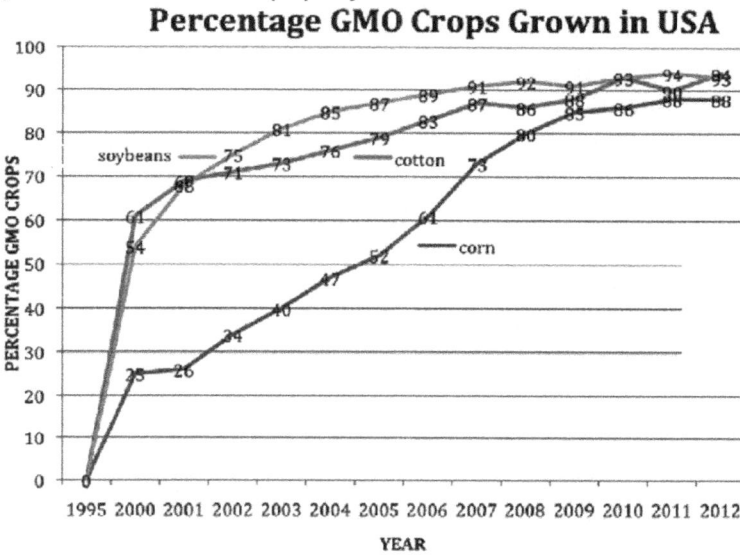

Percentage GMO Crops Grown in USA

Genetically-Modified Organisms in United States Agriculture: Mandate for Food Labeling - Scientific Figure on ResearchGate. Available from: https://www.researchgate.net/figure/Percentage-of-GMO-Crop-Varieties-1996-2012-The-percentage-of-crops-in-the-US-from-GMO_fig1_276493549 [accessed 5 Jun, 2024]

This second graph is the growth of celiac disease over time.

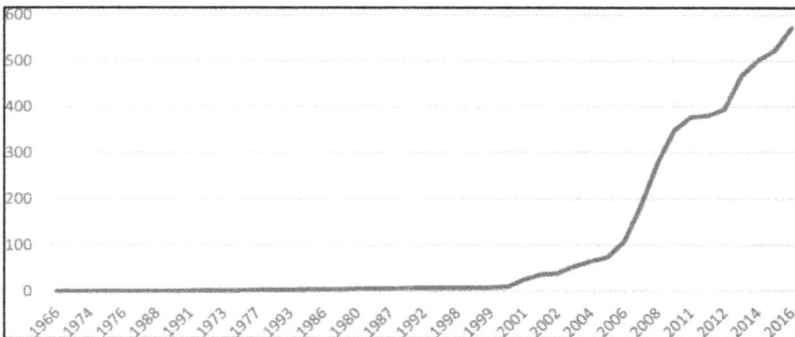

Fueyo-Díaz, R., Magallón-Botaya, R., Masluk, B. et al. Prevalence of celiac disease in primary care: the need for its own code. BMC Health Serv Res 19, 578 (2019). https://doi.org/10.1186/s12913-019-4407-4

Other graphs have some degree of correlation, like the

increase in the use of glyphosate which goes hand and hand with GMO crops because crop tolerance to glyphosate herbicide was quickly genetically inserted into both corn and soybeans. Man was that ever handy for farmers for a while until a bunch of weeds outsmarted us, using biological resistance to ruin easy-peasy. Yes some glyphosate residues are found in many foods and could be the cause of the correlation graphed above, but I don't think glyphosate is used as a desiccant on wheat as much as it has been accused of. And since there are no GMO wheat varieties approved in the USA yet (new one in China in 2024) glyphosate is not used in wheat unless at termination as a desiccant. Other uses of glyphosate on corn and soybeans, I wonder how much they could transfer into the grain, but I'm willing to listen and learn.

Other correlations to the rise of celiac disease do exist. If I were trying to be a smart-Alec, perhaps I could say the increase in celiac disease is attributed to the food trend of Sponge-Bob square pants popsicles that started around the year 2000, but I doubt it. I also doubt celiacs is simply a disease created by a diagnosis or by hypochondriacs. My experience with lyme disease makes me a believer in the significance of these lesser known, sometimes overlooked ailments. Because of these potential food risks, should we look more at differentiating corn and soybean production for food vs. fuel?

Food vs. Fuel debate. I'm a big fan of ethanol but I have cattle buddies who would bop me on the head for saying that. They feel like ethanol has increased their cost to produce beef. Yes, ethanol does initially take about 40% of our corn, then returns quite a bit of cheap livestock feed back to the farm, in the form of dry or wet distillers grains. A pretty neat use of the corn bushel, kicking out 2.9 gallons of fuel ethanol from the starch and then 15-16 lbs. of protein/fat/fiber in a feed byproduct called distillers grains. **Take that math out to an acre of slightly above average Iowa corn at 225 bu/A, that's 650 gal. ethanol and 3500 lbs. of feed, not bad!** About one third of all Dried Distillers Grain gets exported. If we didn't have corn ethanol then would we even be able to support a corn industry in the USA. If we didn't have corn ethanol in gasoline, what would we be paying for gasoline imported from what country? I ask my beef buddies who don't raise corn, if ethanol has raised the value of corn so much, why has corn dipped well below the cost of production numerous times since ethanol became a major player. Obviously, we have the ability to overproduce corn, without ethanol we would have to pay the feedlots to take it.

Ethanol is a success story. The 51 cents blenders subsidy shrunk to 45 cents then was eliminated altogether in 2011, feels like it's been gone forever. The product lives pretty much out there competing for a slice of the fuel market without subsidies, except for my least favorite, the subsidies to the corn farmer through crop insurance and the many aforementioned subsidies handed out to corn farmers via overachieving FSA offices. These subsidies to the farmer however, are not specifically earmarked for ethanol corn, especially since there really isn't an "ethanol only corn vs. a food only corn". I will argue that the positioning for ethanol to be the oxygenate of choice in gasoline through the Renewable fuels standard is good energy policy (policy does not cost taxpayer $) because it is renewable as heck and safe and efficient. Why wouldn't it be good energy policy for a country to use its own renewable fuel to displace oil imported from countries and peoples that don't even like us. Why should we use our military might to police oil fields in some middle eastern nation when we need them on the ready here?

Lifecycle carbon intensity scores on ethanol are 53.3g/MJ vs. gasoline at 98.5g/MJ a 46% reduction for ethanol, that's if the pro-ethanol website I pulled these numbers from used accurate assumptions. They also claimed biogenic tailpipe emissions of CO_2 equals the amount of CO_2 captured by corn plants for a net zero emission. Seems like a good deal for the USA, justifying continued and efficient use of the internal combustion engine, which would take about 100 years to phase this engine type off of my farm.

Let's look at farmer type engines and efficiency. For 30+ years I've been a no-tiller. With all the different planter and tractor configurations I've had, the planter tractor operation itself takes only about half a gallon of diesel fuel per acre. The combine(harvest machine) itself takes about 1.25 gal./A. The efficiency of those internal combustion engines has always impressed me, but those are only two of many trips across the field (sprayer/nitrogen application/dry fertilizer application/ sometimes a lime application/grain cart) and somehow I end up managing to use about 5 gallons diesel/A total on all operations involved in actually growing a corn crop, including trucking it to the local elevator. Gasoline consumption for all the support activities is a bit harder to pin down, but let's just say it is approximately half as much at 2.5 more gallons. So that's 7.5 gallons of "burned by farmer" fuels to get it to an ethanol plant who then cranks 600 gallons of ethanol and 3000+ lbs. of feed out of that acre of average Iowa corn. That nets a lot of fuel (592.5 gals.) after my contribution is removed, to pay for manufacturing and transport of all our inputs and outputs. How in the world could sugar cane derived ethanol shipped clear from South America beat us on Carbon Scores? There has to be an ulterior motive or quid-pro-Joe in there as farmers are witnessing the import of ethanol from our southern competition to satisfy environmental social governance (ESG) scores in order to meet Sustainable Aviation Fuel (SAF) Requirements. I call B.S. on that, and I'll bet 95% of farmers are with me. Are you really going to tell me that after all these years of taxpayer and checkoff dollars investing in experts from government offices and universities, all attempting to improve our resource conservation and efficiency, literal billions spent on environmental programs and cover crop incentives everywhere, yet we are going to buy some flaky theoretical assumptions that makes their ethanol shipped from thousands of miles away, more virtuous than ours! We hope a change of presidents in 2024 could say, "enough already" and bring sanity back. **SAF is a neat new product but should be required to be made with PRODUCT OF USA ethanol and on the diesel side of SAF, they should be required to use Product of USA biofuel sources, not used cooking oil from China.** We ask that our checkoff dollars be used to stop imports of ethanol and imported biofuels.

Speaking of virtue, wouldn't it make sense that our checkoff dollars be spent helping suppliers of farm diesel support the sale and distribution of soy biodiesel or soy biodiesel blends.

15 years ago I had a supplier who basically cut me off of using it just because of the hassle of stocking a separate product. Also, they seemed to fight with it in cold weather due to poor flowability through filters. Can we help them fix this through checkoff money equipment incentives? Then take the next step and promote farmers use this fuel with a top down promotional initiative.

Again it would take some top down leadership to change feed vs. fuel dynamics in this country. Farmers mostly realize that *big yield* years often correlate to *low income* years. We need to rethink that *swinging for the fences* yield strategy and consider getting some base hits with increased foreign and domestic uses. Are we getting enough outside the box thinking and executing out of our multiple check-off investments?

On the environmental virtue side of things, just look at the investment tax payers are unknowingly putting into crop production. You might want to buckle your chin strap, this one could hurt. In conversations with buddies who like to poke at me about the latest and greatest handout at the USDA office, I heard rumors of big USDA payments for cover crops and variable rate fertilizing, both considered to be more environmentally virtuous than standard practices. So I checked with an official NRCS source to confirm. Yes, big money is being handed out. Up to $120/A per year to enroll in a three to five year commitment to use cover crops, and in one state follow the land grant fertilizer maximums and in the other state apply fertilizer using variable rate application. Doing easy math, on every 1000 acres of production, that's $120,000/year or $600,000 total for a five year commitment. Plus it looks like farmers are free to use that money for new equipment purchases, like as in a new seeder (Oh Yes! says the equipment company, glad we paid $20,000 per official for campaign re-election money). $120/A/yr. handout to do a practice that costs the farmer a total $30-40/A to do on his own. I asked the NRCS fellow, where does all this money come from and he said something about the infrastructure bill. We all know the real answer is: from all of our kids' future via a federal government with no self restraint. Can anyone help?

It only adds insult to injury to see all this taxpayer money stuck into virtuous environmental programs, yet we are going to roll over for South American ethanol, while we produce corn for a loss right in our own backyards. Who sold us down the river on this one. Who does our trade deals, Howdy Doody! Where did I put the straightjacket?

From a common sense perspective I don't see how so many people could still be against corn ethanol, it's a slam dunk, a clean burning and efficient fuel source. Most people who have computed gas mileage changes with ethanol also recognize the lower price of ethanol blends more than compensate for changes in gas mileage. I hear the guys on trucking radio at night, banging on ethanol over small engine problems. I don't know what kind of small engines they run that they claim are so sensitive to ethanol. On our farm we have to run chainsaws almost every day in the winter, I run ethanol in them year after year. I don't have trouble with my local 10 or 15% ethanol blended fuel in any small engine, and I've had some of my 4 cycle gas engines for 20 years. The kid's 33 year old wood hauler pickup truck starts at negative 15 Fahrenheit and never has fuel line freeze up on 10 or 15% ethanol blends. Its patented Chevy sponge brakes may not stop it, but it always starts!

Lastly on the corn ethanol promotion side. Ethanol comes to us again next year, and the year after that, and the year after that, and as long as Gretta's dreams of the sun no longer shining stay at bay. It's almost like, renewable. The dino fuels, on the other hand might have a more finite supply, as last I checked, no dinosaurs are roaming the earth anymore. I'll refrain from obligatory jokes about presidents or anything.

As science and time progress, our nation may find it necessary to get real serious about the food vs. fuel vs. feed thing. We can do it, but there is a cost to doing these additional degrees of separation. Maybe we should let the other guys (Brazil & Argentina) be the cheap corn guys since they seem to beat us on that note every year anyway. Maybe **the U.S. corn industry should be the customer driven premium suppliers of world grains.** Identity preserved grains coupled with industry wide *self regulation(cut-the-rate deal)* of N and P fertilizer rates, and we may be able to get a bunch of customers back. The advantage of gene editing and GMO technologies is that this science can be used to make a hybrid not only herbicide resistant but also more appropriate for a specified use as a feed or fuel, or maybe even for a very specific pharmaceutical use. I'm not sure at this time if anything should be used for human food except non-GMO hybrids and/or those varieties of older corns that have been people food for centuries. I think Mexico's consumers and a lot of our former customers would agree with me on this one.

28.

Lessons Learned and Points Pondered While Driving Tractors 670 Miles across the Midwest

I like tractors. I like cows too, but I'd rather drive a couple tractors across the plains than drive a herd of cows. Cowboys used to round up cattle all around this side of the Rockies using various trails to get them to a town like Sedalia, Missouri then walk them all the way to Philadelphia. In Missouri they didn't even have to drive the cows, the cowboys just got ahead of the herd and "showed them" the way....get it, the "Show Me State".

In Ohio we lived near one of those little towns created for the cattle drive. The town was named Midway and strangely enough it had a Sedalia P.O. According to local oral history, the town was on a great cow path. Even though Norm couldn't remember where he left all his gates, he did remember local history and told us the town was named that way because mail from the Sedalia, Missouri post office would be forwarded there, because it was the "midway" point on the cattle drive. I reckon the pony express could take a shorter route than the cattle drive as "ford"ing streams could be "dodge"d by the use of a ferry (you used to be able to call them that).

The town naming theory may not be *just old man talk* either because according to the net, the distance of the first leg would have been 578 miles, while the last leg is 500 miles, and that's by highway. Close enough, aye, could've been entirely different by the way the crow flies. The old men who would tell this story would always make sure they told you about all the services the town had to offer for the cattle drive. Services like blacksmiths, livery stables, general stores, undertakers, hotels, and of course the Sedalia post office where love letters were to show up and if they didn't, there were also bars and brothels. They always had to tell you with a big grin that there were brothels.

One day I stopped through the Sedalia, Missouri historic society expecting to see a big display on the Ohio sister city, but none was to be found. They didn't really believe my story, and said I would have to "show them" some evidence. What am I going to show them, an old horseshoe? They were very skeptical when I submitted the following as hearsay evidence; "I always did notice a disproportionate number of bow-legged slow talking cowboy types hanging around the Ohio sister city." At least one of them ought to be a(n) heritable trait.

Tractors are much faster than cows but much slower than cars, that's why we put slow moving vehicle triangle signs on the back of the tractor or implement we pull, it's not just so young naive car drivers can do stupid stuff around us. You just don't know what to expect from a road until you use it with your particular load. I always think I should have known about a rough patch of road because I've traveled it by car, but a car will often hide it. You could drive your car on any of these roads I'm going to tell you about and you'd think I'm nuts telling you my head and cab roof were close associates. The only state I wouldn't want to drive my own car in is Hawaii, they say its roads are the roughest in the country, plus it's difficult to drive to.

My first trip 670 miles west in a tractor was in a red Case 7220 front assist, about 165 hp using an 8.3 Cummins motor and an 18 speed full powershift transmission with an air launch seat. I was about the third owner of it and at the time it had about 7000 engine hours. Having already used it for about 6 years, I had very much confidence in it. The implements I needed to pull would both be considered wide loads if we hauled them individually on a semi trailer. All state codes allowed for triple towing for motorhome, motorsports recreational vehicles…."farm tractors or motor vehicles towing implements of husbandry"….The plan was to hook my "implements of husbandry" in tandem, a 450 bu. grain cart and then a manure spreader behind that. An immediate problem is the hitch didn't extend far enough out the back of the grain cart, so first I would have to look around for significant enough metal and weld up a hitch extension. Luckily everything I needed was in my metal pile. This was a job I had to do on my own because I thought my local welder buddy would try to talk me out of it. Since I had been dropped off at the Ohio farm by Pittsburgh Pete, a brother in law from of all places, Pittsburgh, a tractor was my only ride back west, short of Amtrak or a buzzard's back. As fate would have it, I was behind the grain cart welding away when a truck pulls up, it's the local welder, he's not going to like this, so I had one of my best lines ever ready for him, "Hairdog, I ain't asking your permission, just your prayers." It still took a while to get him on the same page but when he turned the corner he was all in. I can't even tell you how much that helped bolster my spirit.

While I finished welding he's already wiring in the extension to run the lights on the manure spreader which would be in the rear. Then he calls another buddy of ours to bring the cab cam, a device which would allow me two camera views, one which we shot down on the welded up hitch, the other out the back of the manure spreader so I would know exactly what was going on with cars behind me.

The last thing I needed to load was a bunch of t-posts (steel fence posts) loaded to create a platform in the auger cart so I could lay my mattress taken out of the sleeper in the semi. At 4:00pm on an ugly early spring day I loaded up with fuel, duct taped the clip pins into the hitch pins, double checked the safety chains, kicked all the tires and headed west. Hairdog agreed to observe for a few miles until I got to the seed plant and we'd do a safety check, good place since they were ISO 9001 approved. It all checked out and we said, see ya.

The rig followed me around on the turns way better than

the 52 ft. semi trailers I have pulled, part of that is because it was single axle trailer to single axle trailer and total length 45 ft. combined vs. 60 ft. on semi tractor-trailers. Since the grain cart was wider than the turd hearse, it was a little difficult to judge where to run on the rougher shoulders, the main thing was, I could always be right of the centerline and I could always see when a car needed to pass, I tried to cooperate with a fade right, that rear camera was awesome. It really drove nice and I settled into a slow steady 19 mph. Using two lane roads to move farm equipment in Ohio is challenging, mailboxes are everywhere, the lane width is narrow, shoulders narrow and lots of cars, but the roads were pretty smooth. Thanks to asphalt, the air launch seat was pretty tame.

It never fails when driving a wide load that oncoming cars will meet you right when you get next to a mailbox or road sign. Note to rural drivers; farmers have to weave around stuff that is on our right, so your timing and our timing is like a dance. Sometimes that dance gets screwed up by car drivers actually slowing down too much coming toward us, it's all about timing. Also, it is never safe to pass around us going uphill on a double yellow, a few more minutes and you will usually get a chance with a little fade right by the farmer. Also guard rails suck for us, there is only so much we can do to fade right in a guard rail area or bridge for that matter, so oncoming traffic please be ready to slow down quickly in those kind of choke points. Farmers trying to move equipment in a train of more than three slow moving implements should try to limit this kind of activity because the cars trying to get around us get pretty impatient and mad and I don't blame them, the madder people get the stupider they do. Young drivers of cars please be careful when you see a Slow Moving Vehicle (SMV) triangle sign in front of you, you will be right up on us *before you can get off your phone*!

Also, a technique young drivers can employ when coming toward our wide loads is to stay solid in your lane a little longer than you might want, then begin to fade right just prior to the point where we would meet, so that the "apex of avoidance" would be almost past the point where we would collide, giving the car driver a chance to correct in case the shoulder throws the steering a little wacky. This technique was taught years ago in drivers ed and is also helpful on the nights where a blinding set of any kind of headlights are coming at you. You sure don't want to be caught by that shoulder and over-correct taking you back across the center line before you've passed one another. Sometimes on narrower roads and pinch points all these good ideas simply come down to two strangers just figuring out how to cooperate with one another, and get on with their day.

I angled up though west central Ohio and watched the sun go down somewhere before the Indiana line. The Indiana roads were a bit wider, just as smooth, and I couldn't believe it when I already crossed the I-69 freeway between Indy and Fort Wayne. I wasn't tired yet, but figured it may be my last chance for a truck stop, so I pulled in.

I always feel a little intimidated at truck stops but try wheeling into one with a rig like mine. It made me more than a little self-conscious. There was no way to park without thinking, "This will probably light up channel 19," especially when they see what I'm going to do next!

Unfortunately, there wasn't a dark corner in which to park. Nope, I had to park right under a light, in full illumination. I decided to pull a decoy and walk into the truck stop to get a late night snack and since I had two more days ahead of me, I avoided the sushi bar and the egg salad. I got my mind right during the walk back to the rig and decided to laugh about the sight of me loosening the ratchet on the front of the auger cart tarp, climbing the ladder and squeezing gracelessly like a marsupial infant under it, then jumping down into my makeshift mouse scent infused sleeping arrangement. It was way better than any foxhole, I had a roof, steel walls, a mattress, no one shooting at me, and thanks to the little grain inspection window on the front of the cart, I even had a night light.

I slept like a baby and luckily woke at the crack of dawn, climbed out my marsupial pouch and got outta Dodge before the Muncie news showed up. Notice I did not say I got coffee or mouse tea. Strategically I thought keeping a low tone and empty gut was the best policy as options for getting off the road were not as good as normal. Somewhere along that route is a sign at an old truck stop that says, "Eat here and get gas," which encouraged me to stick with my strategy. State Route 28 in Indiana has always treated us well and takes you straight across the state perfectly into friendly territory in Illinois, the same route Jill and I used on the last Conestoga ride 17 years earlier. I say friendly territory because we were still lucky enough to have friends in Ford County (like Jim and Carol), "where they all drive Chevys," recalling the great Chevy pickup truck ad from either the late 80s to early 90s. My kids still use an awesome '91 Chevy Silverado 1500 to deliver firewood. Their enterprise, *The Moron Firewood Co.*, whose motto has been changed to, "*Where you get a little more-on with every load.*" Obviously they used most of their advertising budget on rear cab glass.

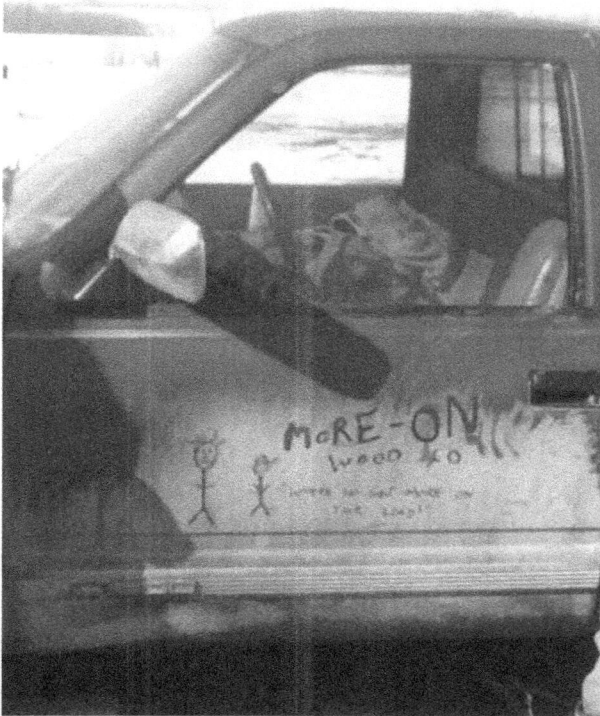

Using U.S. Route 136, another straight shot across a state, I would be driving within 10 miles of a very good friend's farm, whom I won't mention by name because I do not want to incriminate him. I was passing through in the daylight and really wanted to say howdy, so he and his awesome dad met me along the road, brought me some food, checked out my hillbilly R.V., wished me luck and said, see ya.

They saved me big time on wheeling this rig back through another truck stop, or McDonald's drive through. As selfish as it was for me to bother them, just a quick visit like this can do so much for the soul, at least my soul. The dad of my bud once asked me during one of our midwest moves; How did you like your last neighbors? I said real good. He said in turn, "Well then, you'll like your next neighbors."

There seemed to be way less traffic than I expected across 136. I saw some elderly couples probably going to the pharmacy or cashing their Social Security checks, some even driving so slow I had to throttle back. I may have seen an Ag Chemical rep speeding around me, and a bunch of grain tractor trailers hauling the goods to market. The road was almost ridiculously vacant, I found myself checking out all the prosperous farmsteads, bin sites with monstrous bins, grain legs bigger than our elevator in town, pole barns with doors big enough to pull the combine in with the header still on. When you farm, and in essence compete with every one of these farms, the mind can't help but ask, what am I even doing in this business? It seems to have become a rich man's sport. Don't get me wrong, I do not have envy, because many of those farms are juggling more balls than I desire to. There is no doubt, big midwest grain farms are doing well in the 2000s.

I can occupy some of these midwest driving moments looking for even one piece of equipment my grain farm may someday be able to afford used, second, third, or fourth hand. I shouldn't lust over equipment because I'm pretty accustomed to being the last stop before the salvage yard. Maybe that one USDA official knew that, and it explains why he addressed me as "Mr. Salvage." One has to ponder this question, "if the equipment manufacturers knew the USDA was going to let go of subsidies, reverting to free market principles, perhaps even restoring the middle class farm, would they then build a smaller cheaper lower technology combine?" Right now, if the cheapest smallest new combine with heads is say $500,000, I'm assuming the subsidized system is baked into the combine's design. Must we have all the technology ever invented in every new combine. Can't we get out of the cab to set the chaffer and sieve. Can't we use our hands in the cab to steer instead of eating our PB&J sandwiches out of our "in cab" refrigerator. I'm not asking them to make a combine with no seat and no steering wheel, you know, for the farmer who lost his ass and doesn't know which way to turn (another gratuitous farmer joke). I'm just wondering, what would the market ask for in a combine if we had no subsidies. Or, does the equipment also help design the Ag system we play in. Which came first, the chicken or the egg? If you only make combines in the half million dollar up to million plus range, does that drive the farms to be bigger in order to justify the investment? Which came first, the big combine or the big farm subsidies? If you have an open stretch of road and 20 mph to ponder these questions, let me know the answer.

All of this eye candy, yet I still looked forward to a passing grain trailer so I could wave to someone. The last two neighborhoods we lived in would only wave to me with one finger, so it's always nice to find a naive group of wavers.

Illinois unfortunately went upscale on their road design which totally messed me out of my approximate 20 mph average, costing me about 4 mph. Concrete lobbyists must have convinced the legislature to approve concrete shoulders, which may be good for longevity of roads but bad for longevity of loads. That darned expansion joint went clear across the lane then continued on that same line across the shoulder. I felt every joint and occasionally got launched almost to the roof even with no air in the seat. There was no way to escape the expansion joint, it pounded me relentlessly. I started making an effigy of asphalt in my mind, begging for its return, thinking, "it's not my asses fault they used concrete." Maybe it would be a good idea to cut the shoulder joints in between the lane joints, or else just chew the shoulders up entirely and make them into gravel.

Rantoul, Fischer, Heyworth, McLean, San Jose, and finally to my dreaded Illinois river crossing at Havana, Illinois. As the sun was setting I entered Havana city limits, and a town cop started swarming me. He was like a bee buzzing around trying to figure it all out. Every time he got behind me I pulled over a bit to let him know I could see him back there in my camera, but his lights never came on. Believe it or not, I wanted him to pull me over so I could get an escort across the Illinois river bridge or maybe just get somebody to talk to. I remembered that bridge to be a big humpback bridge with narrow lanes. The first and maybe last time I wanted to be pulled over by a cop.

Unfortunately, he left me all alone. Now it's just me vs. bridge. The bridge was in front of me before I knew it, no way to see all the way across it because it humped up so much, probably a half mile across. I took a quick gage on lane width and tire clearance, not much to work with. If I put my auger cart tire against the curb the other would be snug up to the center-line. The curb and the bridge iron seemed only a foot apart, no room for error. Luckily it was just dark enough everyone would have lights on and I could flash mine to warn approaching vehicles to slow down. Surely everyone traveling that area has seen a tractor before. I get near the mountain top of the bridge and wouldn't you know, here comes a set of headlights, so I flashed them....with my lights.... crowded over to the curb and stopped forward progress as luckily no one was behind me. The on-coming car driver slowed down and did good and it was off to the races again and safely off the bridge. How do farmers around there do it, it must require an escort for most rigs of today's size.

Now I could pucker down, but still had to concentrate on not letting down too much. I never know how far adrenaline will sustain or how hard I will crash coming off of it. Will I make it to Macomb or not? I'll need to be on top of my game there because I'll have to go through the town, no bypass done yet, is it even in the plans?

Seemed like no time at all and I'm coming up on Macomb, so my adrenaline pumps me up again and I went through the whole town without hardly seeing a car. Not far west of Macomb comes a stretch of 4 lane, it was so deserted it was almost spooky. Reminded me of U.S. 50 out in western Utah and Nevada except no 2000 foot mountain ranges, sagebrush, UFOs and/or experimental military aircraft. But I kept an eye to the sky anyway not wanting to be surprised again by a stealth or osprey, like my high school buddy and I experienced on that route (U.S. 50) back in mid-Dec. '89. We were heading for California, cruising right along, middle of the night in a '65 Mustang 200 straight six, no turbo. He had just taken over a night shift of driving and I was trying to sleep with one eye open to watch the speedometer which seemed unbelievably mis-calibrated for the 60 mph we were going. He pokes me and says, "Savage, check this out." A hovering craft with a lot of lights was right in front of us; he said the lights just came on suddenly when we got close. It didn't move and I don't remember a sound, but I think I said hammer down, not being sure how much hammer was left.

I would not swear to it that there was no sound generated by this object because the Mustang was a convertible with two slashes cut by a thief through the canvas behind those little rear wing windows. The slashes were duct taped from the inside and the outside. It was a really good job of taping using color matching tape, but it just couldn't stick forever as it was only 100 mile per hour tape. If you added our 60 mph with a 41 mph opposite vector wind, boom, there goes my tape job. Add in a few whistles around the top, road noise coming through the shifter boot, squeaks from long worn doors, the heater fan chirping on high, it's no wonder the object hung around silently. Did I mention we bought out all the throat lozenges at that one gas station we found across there; can you say, "A little drafty"?

Back to the military test plane. It was like going under a football stadium of lights, well maybe not that big. I think I remember looking behind us to see if they were following but can't remember even seeing it back there at all, makes you question your sanity. Years later I saw Rob at a wrestling reunion and asked him if we really saw that thing, he took a deep breath and said, "we sure did," and that was about the end of that conversation. I could have sworn I saw gills open on the side of his head when he took that breath!

We later figured those guys flying for our side must love screwing around with a lone car in the deserted desert (hey, that's where that word comes from!) Guess that's the kind of stuff that goes through your mind at 20 mph.

By the time I got done hashing through old memories I was in the Mississippi River bottoms pumping myself up to cross it. It's probably about midnight. The bridge at Keokuk is awesome and a piece of cake to cross, but Keokuk itself can be a bit of a challenge. Up 218 to Iowa State Route 2 was the trek ahead. I've crossed the mighty muddy by the end of the second day. Man I was starting to let down, where's a truck stop when you need one!

I can't remember exactly where it was, but I found a nice wide spot on the shoulder near some population. It was rough gravel rutted up from heavy truck parking. Looked like a safe place to get some sleep. As I crawled out of the tractor, through the marsupial pouch to my comfortable bed, I heard a car or two go by, no problem I thought. Next thing I knew I'm waking up to a semi-truck extravaganza, figuring some factory must have sent out a shipment or maybe a new shift coming in, whatever it was I couldn't sleep, so I crawled back in my tractor and it's off to the races again. I figured I got 15 minutes of sleep but somehow I was a new man. So I tuned the radio into late night A.M. and Coast to Coast was talking about the orbit of the massive hidden planet X (Nibiru) and how its magnetic force-field energy was going to cause a pole shift, weather related calamities, climate change, changes in where our food is grown, and these 400 mile long "derecho" winds. What is this all about? Who ever heard of 400 mile long irrational winds? Eleven years later I now understand those winds and darned if our Iowa farm hasn't been on the receiving end of that kind of wind two years in a row now. I looked it up, a "derecho" is technically 58 mph or higher winds for a stretch of 240 miles of continuous storm path damage. Could this be Planet X and not climate change? Needless to say, I was on the edge of my seat listening to this fascinating topic, wondering if the farmland we bought in Iowa may end up pole shifting clear to the equator, maybe I'll get to find that S.O.B. who designed my old Ford Cabover.

All of a sudden I'm going through the Shemik Forest in southeastern Iowa, the largest contiguous forest system in the state. Dark as the ace of spades and as abandoned as the plains of Mongolia. The darkness was so strong, the stars yielded. The Case seemed to love that kind of night so we drifted through it together, man and machine bonding. Guess that's what you do at 500 miles into a voyage with your tractor, how lucky am I.

Farmington, Iowa. I know there is a gas station right along the road. I've gotten a snack and gas there before, probably only a year ago. Should have room to pull off, grab a little sleep and rustle up some grub, maybe even fuel up t'morning (that's "tomorrow morning" a favorite conjugate of one of our illiterate kids). I can make it, but I'm fading fast. I started pulling nose hairs to gain a few more miles each pull, then finally the dim lights of a fading midwest town broke through the darkness, alleluia! Farmington, Iowa!

I'm thinking it was around 2:00 in the morning when I got into my plush bed, the flags from metal t-posts never felt so good as I crawled around in that spacious auger cart to find my mattress. Night John Boy, night Mary Ellen.

It was an awesome rest of the night's sleep. Daylight was already starting when I woke to look out my grain window. I had a real desire for anything that resembled food, especially if it was a chocolate little donut in a bag. I took a spare tums out of my pocket and brushed my teeth with it and jumped up to the top and wedged out of my tarp like I was on an Olympic pommel horse, got my technique refined, third and last night hopefully, nailed it, 9.99s should be the judges scores. Started booking it down the ladder only to look over at people who were watching me through the picture window of a restaurant. What restaurant? I thought this was a gas station and quickie store. I looked around, am I at the right place, is this Farmington, does it even matter, I can get a real breakfast here, yippie! I couldn't tell if anyone was laughing at me and who could blame them, bet they'd have really coughed in their coffee mugs if Jill would have popped out behind me! Anyway, from 40 foot off I could at least tell the patrons were curious. Should I just leave the area, or have the courage to face my peers. A belly growl answered that question.

That was a really fun breakfast until the end. The early birds wanted to get off to choring with a new story to tell, the old farmers were in no hurry cause they wanted the "rest of the story," the townies were getting in later wondering what they missed. I was not to be deterred at first so I made sure I got my sausage biscuits and gravy w/eggs ordered since mush, goetta and hominy, were not on the menu. It's the only meal I might get for the day depending on how the last 150 miles goes. I noticed the young men kind of hanging on for a few minutes until they figured it out, I didn't want to hold up chores, so I started talking. They were not scornful but curious which direction and how far I was going, how far did you come. There may have even been the need to verify that I was not moving into their own home turf. I figured real quick, these guys are just like me, they're constantly calculating for authenticity & trustworthiness, like Regan with Gorbachev, "trust but verify."

Eventually most of the curiosity was satisfied and next I'm stuck with a know-it-all, Debbie Downer. But this was the guy version, we'll just call him Dennis Downer. He proceeded to give me a tongue lashing for even daring to pull two implements like that because it was against the law, according to him, I wouldn't make it out of the county without being arrested. I told him to tell that to the cop back in Havana, Illinois because I wanted him to pull me over and for some reason he wouldn't. At this point the old men stepped in and did intervention saying, "Oh Dennis, you're just full of horse crap; that's just for wagons full of grain pulled behind pickups, it's not even for tractors" or "that only applies to wagons if your truck bed was also considered to be loaded." I wasn't sure anyone knew exactly what the law was, but those biscuits and gravy were so good I could maybe use another. I really appreciated the old fellows' help, they are my heroes. Afterward, one of the last younger guys leaving said in a quiet voice, "Don't worry about Dennis, he does this all the time." What a compassionate thing for a guy to do for a stranger. I noticed Dennis Downer sat there all by himself, probably reading the police blotter, kind of sad.

It seemed like there was something different about the bridge on the west end of Farmington, maybe it was new. I remember looking for that cop Dennis promised me, but I kept going and it seemed no one would stop me, not even just to talk. It was great to be back up to 20+ mph, not because the road was smoother but because the shoulder was gravel. Put those duals out on that big old wide gravel shoulder and roll! Maybe that's what I really always liked about Iowa, the first state heading west to give you some space on the roads and generous shoulders. Big rights-of-way, town squares with some room, people that actually wave to strangers on the road, with all their fingers. I've got to say, State Route 2 in Iowa is my favorite road because of all this.

I feel more comfortable in this country because it has retained the mid-size farm, seems more down to earth and real economy to me. Since I know "the rest of the story" of midwest agriculture I know this is more like it would be were the USDA less of an influence. I'm looking out my tractor window at cow/calf country now, not nearly as subsidized and false economyish as much of midwest grain country I just exited. What is the end game for a farm the size of many midwest Grain Farms, the 3% that farm 50% of row crops, too big for kids to buy them out, they are now destined for corporate buyout. What corporations will it be, seed companies, fertilizer companies, equipment companies, foreign companies, Bill Gates companies or some other corporation that needs offsets for environmental social governance (ESG) scores? Will they get subsidies too? Is it already too late to fix it? Should we even care to fight or just cash in and check out?

A flat tire or blown radiator hose will bring your thoughts around to Realville in a hurry so my fingers were crossed and my mind fixed on willing this thing to a successful conclusion. The few extra miles/hour gained in Iowa seemed to make the miles just disappear, all of a sudden I'm getting close enough to get help from people I know, usually costing me twice as much as help from a total stranger.

Looks like 35 engine hours is going to be the tally on this first trip, averaging about 19 mph. Fuel consumption was ~4 gal./hour costing me approximately 167 gallons at $3.00/gal., that's about $500. If you're curious about miles per gallon, at a shade over 4 MPG, which is a little less fuel efficient than a semi which is in that 5-6 MPG range with a wind catching load like this. Again, this would have been two wide loads on a semi which would have cost $3300/load and maybe some shippers up to $5,000/load. So what is my time worth? Engine hours on a tractor this size might be $120/hour, tire wear is a big question mark. If I were a land grant economist I'm sure I could talk myself out of this trip, because somehow the math of *opportunity cost* would not work. My checkbook however, looked at this trip a lot differently, it saw out of pocket costs being $500 vs. at least $6600, on a tractor I already had bought and paid for! Now that's a no brainer, the way my brain is wired.

Of course I was curious about tire wear, so I asked Hairdog (the Ohio Welder) to give me an estimate of remaining tire tread before leaving Ohio. He estimated about 35% remaining. So the tires were pretty worn out to begin the trip. I'm guessing they were the original Firestone 23 degree tread and had almost 7000 hours on them, the rubber was pretty hard and a little dry checked, but still beautiful in my eyes. I'm a no-tiller – tires last forever. When I got to central Illinois, I noticed my friends were pretty concerned about tire wear and I visually checked them only to notice very little wear. I believe their concern to be warranted had the tires been newish, but my tires were old and now made of hard rubber.

When I dropped the manure spreader off to the local welding shop in Iowa, for some professional repairs to the beaters, I asked his opinion on % tire tread remaining, his estimate was 40%. So I have just gained 5% tread on my Firestones by driving 670 miles! Needless to say, I was thrilled, and even ran on those tires another 1000 hours, but they could get a little slippery on hillsides, turning hillsides into hillslides when you caught some fresh manure.

Because of this "tire gain" hypothesis I was more encouraged to test it out on a set of Goodyear tires fitted to my Case MX 210, the next year. This time it was a single implement I was pulling, my 40' long, end transport Kinze planter, with all my no-till "bling" attached. The tires fared about the same as the trip with the first tractor, they were just as tired, hard and worn, about 40% tread on either end of the trip but no documented gain this time. Again, they lasted about another 1000 hours after the 670 mile trip. The planter tires have this slotted rib and were pretty fresh, but wore surprisingly well going from 75% down to 70% approximately. Hope that helps satisfy someone's curiosity, and maybe you can relate to tire range anxiety if you drive a Tesla.

This second tractor drive seemed to be less of an endurance test. I cut a few engine hours off, down to 32 hours. Speed averaged over 21 mph, faster tractor, but the fuel was about the same total consumption because this awesome tractor drinks a little more fuel/hr. than the older one, 185 hp vs. 165 hp. The advantage of my Mx 210 was the cab size. If I twisted myself just right I could sleep on the floorboard. It wasn't bad if you don't mind a clutch pedal in your ribcage, which was easily fixed with the handyman's secret weapon (duct tape) the second and third night. Truck stops were more negotiable since it's easier to back up one trailer than two. Every morning when you'd get out to stretch back into a normal shape the truckers must have been like, "Hey Mother, looky there, it's a walking c-clamp!"

Thankfully everything went well for the planter trip also, except for losing one box lid probably on a rough bridge seam. It felt good to be finally home, and hopefully no more tractors to drive across a third of the country. I've caught plenty of duff over the years for driving my tractors to move to a new farm, and I'll be the first to admit, this is not normal. Yes, I could have hired truckers to do all of this. But, in a world where you can't print money and you can't borrow on your kids' future, the checkbook has to pay all the bills, and all the bills have to be paid, how else am I to roll? Tragic or comic it's all economic.

29.

Concluditopia

Perhaps the perspective gained from a 20 mph tractor drive on two lane roads in the heart of the midwest is a gift I did not bargain for. In my gut I've always felt like these drives into the western midwest get me further into freedom's last frontier. We can call it the Heartland, Flyover Country, the Land Between the Coasts, whatever you want to call this area whose significance was protected by our founding fathers (via an electoral college), in reality it's simply rural America. Even with a diminishing rural population, we are still an important political force.

In reality, as you can see in the Map below of the 2020 election, rural America exists everywhere, in almost every state, and we make a stand every election for a less intrusive government; voicing our strong desire for freedom. The talking heads and control freaks in the liberal press portray us as the unwashed masses who develop cult followings for an individual leader, when deep down inside they know we would never put our trust in a man over an ideal. An ideal inspired by God that was unique to the founding of this country....liberty.

2020 County Presidential Election Results

County Vote Percentage
- Trump 55% +
- Trump 50-54%
- Trump LT 50%
- Biden LT 50%
- Biden 50-54%
- Biden 55% +

Author Gregg Smith, state data as of 15 December 2020

https://www.linkedin.com/pulse/county-map-2020-presidential-election-gregg-smith-phd-

Rural America is voting to preserve a nation with its own identity, an identity founded on the guarantee of liberties for the individual, that people can pursue their own interests (God given) without tyranny from government. That's just what we were doing moving our farm west, exercising our liberty. Thank God we still have rural America....and soldiers and sheriffs willing to fight to preserve our liberties as defined in the constitution.

As I mentioned earlier, many grain farms are sized to where the grain bins and elevator legs are bigger than our local elevator that serves probably 50 grain/cattle farms. Some of these setups are beautiful, and make me think of the dynasties or empires of the old country Europe, with the beautiful castles that are reminders of a past that our country fought the Revolutionary War to reject. The people who founded this country not only sought religious freedom but also freedom from tyranny. Something about castles makes me think tyranny and a bunch of peasants were involved. I suspect tyranny was exercised through taxation, like say your taxes are used to build the castle (yes, USDA gives low interest long term loans for grain bins

215

---

setups). Well, as a tax paying freeman, I say enough already, let's figure out how to end farm subsidies, before the peasant population grows any more. The USA was not designed to work on a system of haves and have-nots, we must find a better way to do *no more harm to the middle class farm.*

On tyranny. Can tyranny be conducted by simply designing a system where those who **don't** play within the system wither on the vine? Could it be some kind of soft tyranny to design a system where 3% of U.S. farms control almost half of all U.S. row crop production. We know this is bad for rural America, isn't it also bad for food security?

Do we really need a Farm Bill? Do we really need subsidies for smart millionaires?

Maybe we need a wake-up call in Rural America. We cannot blame our country's economic woes solely on urban culture issues. The policies we have accepted are plenty enough to blame, at least financially. To illustrate that point, see the map below, which shows an imbalance in per capita spending which makes rural red states look like a bigger drain on per capita fiscal budgets than blue states. Just because we know some of this imbalance is a result of infrastructure cost divided by fewer people, we also know the ridiculousness of some programs, especially the ones managed by the USDA, many of them I've tried to expose in this book.

Agritopia

Washington DC, Wyoming, and Alaska had the highest rates of federal funding per person.

Federal funding per capita by state, 2020

Map Table

$1.8K $7.0K

Source: US Census Bureau

https://usafacts.org/articles/which-states-rely-the-most-on-federal-aid/

How to change the system? I hope I can help with the information within these pages. Change probably has to start by changing our own cynicism toward the system and politicians. It is not really a bottom up system we have here, it has been very top down for decades. That does not mean we have to give up, but we do need to wise up. We have to quit thinking we are being represented by our big farm groups, they have been selling the middle class farm down the river for decades, checkoff programs included. I've been pretty hard on our farm state Congressmen, but how are they going to know our opinions, if all they hear from is the Farm Bureau or the biggest commodity checkoff groups, so call Congress and go to the town hall meetings and speak truth to power. We need

217

our Congressmen and Congresswomen to help, without them we get nowhere. I suggest that you speak your opposition to mainstream farm programs early in any public meetings so that those who are also there to challenge the status-quo are encouraged and not made timid by "meeting uni-think". Remember you are not alone. I believe it to be a waste of effort to think you can change these big lobbying groups from within, it would be like turning an aircraft carrier in the local lake's marina, you're better off speaking your own truth individually to our elected officials in Congress.

Other countries are driving their tractors (Feb. 2024) creating road blockades because of various problems, most having to do with fuel policies and excessive paperwork due to over regulation as a result of European "green environmental" policies. Some of this same "green" policy, like determination of a "carbon intensity score" is staring us right in the face. How will we respond? How we respond probably depends on how trapped we feel. Also, more government subsidies equals more leverage which means more trapped. Apparently the European farmers feel trapped enough that a protest becomes necessary. The U.S. should learn from the European farm problems and reject the same kind of onerous policies that brought their farmers to a breaking point.

We are all left with individual choices. Just like I was reminded many times in a phone call with one of my favorite USDA authorities (because she treated me respectfully, R...E...S...P...E...C...T...!); "participation in any USDA program is voluntary." I will agree with her to a point, but try competing for land in a neighborhood where all the land has dozens of different USDA programs (including CRP or CREP) and subsidies mainstreamed and baked into the price. Try securing an operating loan when the loan officer says you will need 75+% crop revenue insurance, then you have to buy it at an unsubsidized ridiculously high price. Try competing for cash rent as an unsubsidized purchaser of catastrophic insurance against someone locking in maximum revenue protection then shuffling bushels to make it pay, playing the crop insurance game to the hilt. The USDA employees can say all they want that "participation is voluntary" but they all know the reality is, our survival within the system they created makes participation almost mandatory, resulting in a very un-American business model.

Even within "their" system some things can be done voluntarily. We can all voluntarily choose to help that young family get a start on a farm, without going to the USDA office, for a "special young farmers program". It could be as simple as helping to involve young kids in livestock ownership and care. Let the livestock help raise the child, instead of the village people. I cannot even tell you how much free parenting my wife and I have gotten out of livestock, especially goats. I have to remind myself that the most valuable crop we raised on all these farms is a family. The farm is a good place to raise kids, hardships and all, teaching kids that everything to learn in life is not on a cell phone or internet feed. Even absentee landowners can recognize the value of more families in these communities. Holding onto an old building site with a barn and a feedlot floor might be 5 acres less cash rent for you, but a world of opportunity for a young family. A break on cash rent can voluntarily be given to those who really do a good job of soil conservation, using no-till, contouring, buffer strips, cover crops and waterways. Conservation costs money. All landowners should be responsible for conservation, this is not the government's job, besides they've proven to suck at it! To put a number on the true cost of conservation on tillable midwest farmland would start for me at $40/A/yr. I might not even see the return within my lifetime but my kids and grandkids will.

Plenty of tough gritty young men and women in their 20s and 30s are interested in farming but see capital expenditure as an overwhelming barrier. The USA can be proud and rest assured, we do not have a lack of desire to live an agrarian lifestyle, but simply lack the financial opportunity. I really think the HFSA can help, if we can just get it done.

Tens of thousands of Farmers and Ranchers want to find a way out of feeling trapped in a web of governance by USDA programs and carbon/environmental programs. Thankfully, we have not gotten to the third party monthly farm inspections like some European countries attempted....yet! Government should not design winners and losers, a free market meritocracy should. We could all use your help to overhaul our broken agriculture. Help can come from all farming and non-farming, taxpaying, God fearing Americans to undo this onerous system and give us a less cluttered pathway to make our living in rural America. We need to diminish the USDA's presence in rural America and on our farms. No Farm bill necessary. The HFSA coupled to unsubsidized catastrophic crop insurance could be the path back to a more free market system. A path back to more middle class farms. A path back to more people fulfilling their own version of Agritopia.

Again, the Capital switchboards will help you find your U.S. House and Senate Leaders @ 202-224-3121. Don't be afraid to speak truth to power.

I give you one last story given to me in the barnyard. I have to bottle feed this one calf that was a twin, momma cow simply would not let her feed. She will flat chase you down to get that morning feeding. I keep her in the pen with a big bull. There they stand side by side this morning at the gate, 1600 lbs and 80 lbs. The calf starts gulping down the milk replacer like it's her last meal and the bull does what a bull does and swings his massive head down low and gives the calf a good bump like, "get outta here, I might be needing this spot if farmer Dave gives me a flake of hay!" The little calf was not to be deterred and she would not let go of the bottle. The bull came around for a second blow and that little calf took it but leaned into him assertively. She leaned in enough that you could say she was pushing him as he withdrew, all the while not losing contact with that glorious milk. The third blow might put an end to this contest, but it did not come as the bull stepped back from the calf in a show of respect I suppose. I did not scold the bull or poke the bull because he obviously read the situation correctly and backed off. By now this calf is getting enough respect from me to earn a name, "STAY-SEE" immediately came to mind. I butcher the spelling because you "see" she obviously wanted to just "STAY" doing what she was doing, bull be damned "this is my space, cut it out!" If Esop had this story in fable form, he would attempt a moral. Perhaps it would be: If the bull is poking at your worthy efforts to sustain yourself, try leaning into him.

Hopefully, with this appeal from the trenches we can fire up an honest and serious debate over farm and rural policy, not just a conversation with no action attached. We are going to need help from the top to achieve change.

One of my favorite farm slogans is "will work for food." I want to thank the consumers of the commodities grown here in rural America. From this farmer's perspective, you feed us!

Forty years of observing. Four winters of writing. I'm done now.